A JOHN CATT PUBLICATION

Leadership Matters

How leaders at all levels can create great schools

By Andy Buck

with
Oli Tomlinson
James Toop

LEADERSHIP
MATTERS
With You, For You

First Published 2016

by John Catt Educational Ltd,
12 Deben Mill Business Centre, Old Maltings Approach,
Melton, Woodbridge IP12 1BL

Tel: +44 (0) 1394 389850 Fax: +44 (0) 1394 386893
Email: enquiries@johncatt.com
Website: www.johncatt.com

© 2016 Andy Buck

All rights reserved.

ISBN: 978 1 909717 90 9

Set and designed by John Catt Educational Limited

Praise for *Leadership Matters*

"Andy's latest book is a masterpiece, combining the vast expertise and experience he gained as a teacher and school leader with his extensive knowledge of the most useful theory and research into leadership." Brian Lightman, former general secretary of ASCL

"A very powerful tool in the hands of school leaders who are determined to do the best for young people." Chris Husbands, Vice Chancellor, Sheffield Hallam University and former Director of UCL Institute of Education

"This book is an important contribution to the mission we all need to commit to: developing school leaders of the present and the future." Emma Knights, Chief Executive, National Governors Association

"'I cannot think of a more useful book on school leadership. It is full of good sense and practical suggestions, with a strong theoretical underpinning." John Dunford, former general secretary of the Association of School and College Leaders

"Alive with real examples, this book is – unusually – both an easy-to-apply practical guide and a stimulus for new thinking and fresh possibilities." Jon Coles, Chief Executive of United Learning

"Rarely will you see the complexities of leadership and management made this clear and translated into a book this useful. Each school leader and would-be-leader should pick up a copy." Alex Quigley, Director of Learning and Research, Huntington School, author of *The Confident Teacher*

"A must read for school leaders. Comprehensive and packed full of evidence and practical wisdom on the characteristics of successful leaders." James Toop, CEO Teaching Leaders

"Typically accessible, with practical advice and some excellent analysis and personal insights it is a useful resource for reading in chunks as and when or in one sitting as you prepare for a new challenge. It made me wince and nod within the same chapters as I recognised my traits, successes and mistakes." Professor Toby Salt, CEO, Ormiston Academies Trust

"This is an invaluable resource for school leaders not only in the UK but from further afield – highly recommended." Susan Douglas, Senior Adviser, Schools, British Council and CEO, Eden Academy

"Andy Buck has created an easy-to-read yet immensely powerful guide for every school leader, a book filled with wisdom, humour and practical guidance. He manages to reach a perfect balance: a mix of inspiration with occasional uncomfortable truths to confront. This is a must-read." David Weston, Chief Executive, The Teacher Development Trust

"A clear and compelling argument that collaboration within our schools and across schools fosters strategic thinking and healthy reflection." Jill Berry, Leadership Consultant, author

"Andy Buck has been there and done it and this book is evidence of that, bringing together a range of leadership thinking and practical in-school experience that delivers a practical,useful handbook for school leaders everywhere." John Campbell, Executive Director, Growth Coaching International,Sydney, Australia

Contents

For Barbara

There has never been, nor will there ever be, anything quite so special as the love between the mother and a son.

Unknown

Foreword

There really is no job like leading a school, no better way to make a difference that lasts through the generations. It is a test of character, confidence, strategy and delivery. The education sector is a restless one and the determination to improve standards for children never stops. The current passion for debate on education and leadership that we see daily across social networks shows how our current leaders think about their role and their impact.

Andy Buck is a highly credible leader in his own right. His work to establish teaching schools as one of the key delivery mechanisms for school improvement is testimony to his impact. He understands leadership from the classroom onwards and his advice and guidance is rooted in reality. I have worked alongside Andy and know the value and inspiration he brings to school leaders.

This latest book from Andy comes at a time when the leadership landscape has changed dramatically. We need now, more than ever, leaders who understand the power of collaboration, both within a single school or across a group of schools, leaders who can work together to create a brilliant education system for all the children in this country. In other words, 'Leadership Matters.'

This is a book for leaders at any level. Whether you are a middle leader, senior leader, head teacher or system leader responsible for more than one school, the principles that underpin great leadership are similar. To be a great leader you need to know yourself and those around you. Above all you need to understand the context of the team, the community and the schools in which you lead so that the actions you take as a leader are the right ones. There is not one best way, no universal strategy for success; judgement is crucial. The best decisions are rooted in clear values and thoughtful analysis and are made in search of the very best outcomes for young people.

'Leadership Matters' combines sound theory with authentic experience and credible evidence. This is a book which is full of real life examples and anecdotes from someone who has been on a leadership journey from head of department to headship to becoming a Director at the National College of Teaching and Leadership. The complex art of leadership is demystified in a book which is readable, full of humour and packed with insightful suggestions.

This book will inspire and encourage leaders whatever stage of the journey they are on. Above all, it will reaffirm the sheer joy and privilege of leading a school and the importance developing great leaders both for now and for the future.

Russell Hobby

General Secretary, National Association of Head Teachers
May 2016

Introduction

Never doubt that a small group of thoughtful,
concerned citizens can change the world.
Indeed, it is the only thing that ever has.
Margaret Mead

When I started teaching geography in a north London comprehensive school back in 1987, I was passionate about my subject. I had been in training for a year at the Institute of Education in London and had learnt a huge amount from my inspirational tutors, Frances Slater and David Lambert. I loved the pupils in my school and I loved my job. But even then, I knew how my own success depended upon others around me. There were times when I needed to draw on more experienced colleagues in the school when dealing with difficult pupils. If our pupils were to have a coherent and challenging educational experience that enabled them to achieve great things, there needed to be proper planning and organisation of the curriculum as a whole. If I was to continue to grow and develop as a teacher, I needed the chance to work with others in a productive and focused way that enabled me to reflect on my practice and improve. In other words, even then, I knew that I needed to be working as part of a well-orchestrated team: that leadership mattered.

These days, of course, it is pretty widely accepted that second to the quality of teaching itself, the single thing that makes the biggest difference to outcomes for pupils is leadership. So this book isn't about *why* leadership in schools matters. It is about what great leadership *looks like* at all levels, both within schools and beyond them. It unashamedly aims to cover leadership in a huge range of contexts. As a school leader reading this, you may be at the beginning of your own leadership journey, taking your very first steps into middle leadership. You may be a senior leader or the head of a school. You may even be a system leader with a role working across more than one school, leading a federation or an alliance of schools.

From my experience, whilst the focus of your work as leader will undoubtedly shift according to your role, many of the key elements of great leadership are present at every level, regardless of your experience or sphere of influence. All that differs is your context. To say otherwise, in my view, is to over-complicate the issue. Great leadership is the same, however senior you happen to be. What matters most is how you apply that understanding of your situation to be able to focus your leadership actions and approach to suit your context. For example, a brand new head of English or leader of literacy across a school needs to quickly assess the capacity of the teachers delivering this important curriculum area before deciding what the team needs to do next as well as how, as a leader, they should approach making this change happen. If capacity and expertise is low, the right approach may very well be pretty directive. On the other hand, if the team is experienced and highly competent, such an approach is likely to backfire. This is no different from a head taking over a new school working out what the strategic priorities need to be over the next 3-5 years and how best to implement them. The only difference is the scale.

So the approach of this book is to take an evidence-based look at what great school leadership looks like and allow you to translate this into the context you are working in. My own experience has shown me the power of this approach, particularly in recent years, where my work has given me a privileged insight into hundreds of schools. Where a school or group of schools sees the value of leaders collaborating together, with a shared set of values, goals and ways of working, there is no limit on the outcomes for pupils, so long as leaders can take their agreed shared approaches and modify them to suit their situation.

In thinking about what makes a great school, I have drawn heavily on my learning from the time I was leading the London Challenge *Good to Great* (G2G) programme. This books aims to synthesise that learning with my knowledge and experience of school leadership more generally, drawing on examples from the schools I have worked in and had the pleasure to work alongside over the last 30 years. It aims to break down this learning into discrete, easily digestible chunks. For each area, I will map out the opportunities and challenges you may well be facing right now in your current role, providing you with useful theory and background to help you bring out the best in you and those around you.

To allow you to apply this learning in your context, I will use the terms team, colleagues or staff quite a lot. These can mean different things, depending on your situation, so feel free to apply these as appropriate:

Middle leaders: When I use this term, I am usually referring to those staff that are in the team you lead or upon whom you rely for delivery if you have a whole-school responsibility.

Senior leaders: When I am talking about your team, colleagues or staff, I am usually referring to those you line-manage or upon whom you rely to deliver your whole-school responsibility. This may include all staff at times.

Heads: (and for heads, read principals or heads of school) In the context of these phrases, they are usually referring to the members of your senior team. It may sometimes also refer to middle leaders and the wider staff team.

System leaders: as someone who is running more than one school, in this context your colleagues are likely to be the heads of each school and sometimes the senior teams in each. Occasionally it will refer to all the staff in all your schools.

Governors and/or trustees: depending on your context, these terms may relate to the single governing body of your school, the board of trustees of your multi-academy trust or federation or the 'local' governance for one school within a multi-academy or federated group of schools. In whichever context, these references are about the important oversight and vital contribution such governance provides.

Similarly, when I talk about **schools**, I am using the word generically to include all schools, academies, free schools, special schools and colleges who are educating pupils from early years to aged 19.

It is also worth mentioning that, whilst I have just separated out the four different levels of leadership to make it quite explicit that the book is written with all four in mind, in my view, the more that a school thinks of its leadership capacity existing within a single leadership team, the better. It may sound like I am contradicting myself, but my point is this: all leaders in any school need to feel they are part of a single leadership effort, with a shared set of values and ways of working. Otherwise, you end up with frequent misunderstanding and unproductive tensions. You also lose the opportunity for more senior leaders to coach and mentor their less experienced colleagues with the same goals and ambitions in mind. It's why, when I work with schools on leadership development, I won't work with groups of middle leaders unless all the senior leaders in the school are involved too. Experience has taught us that if senior leaders aren't part of this shared experience, the process has significantly reduced impact, not just because senior leaders don't have access to the language and concepts discussed, but because there is a 'them and us' culture that just gets in the way.

You as a leader

Part 1 of the book provides an opportunity for you to reflect on your personal qualities. What is the moral purpose and motivation that sits behind your approach? Who are you as a leader? How do you tend to respond in certain situations? How well do you know yourself and how able are you to manage your emotions? How do you respond when the going gets tough? These personal characteristics will have a strong influence over your effectiveness every single day. School leaders are not immune from basic things going wrong. When you have a tough day and, if you teach, one of your own lessons has been a bit of a disaster or you have had a really challenging and unsuccessful meeting with a difficult member of staff, how you manage your own emotions and remain positive is tough. Your staff need you to remain optimistic in such situations, even when there appears to be absolutely no reason to do so!

For all leaders, having a strong sense of one's own personal characteristics is a hugely powerful and affirming base from which to lead, particularly when the challenges of a school leadership role have the potential to become all-consuming.

Your situation

Part 2 of the book is all about the importance of context. This is probably the moment to consider what I have named the 'giraffe concept'. From an early age, like me, you have probably learnt that the reason that giraffes have evolved to have long necks is so they can reach the leaves on trees that other animals can't reach. The long neck is the key thing that enables them to be successful and it's the same for them all. But a quick look at giraffes across the world reveals that, whilst they may all share similarly long necks, their markings can vary considerably. Some are dark, some lighter. Some have large patches of colour, some smaller. The markings vary according to their environment and the age of the giraffe. They have evolved to suit their context. For me, the same principle applies to school leadership. As a leader, you need to be clear what are the leadership *long neck* issues: the things about leadership you need to know and understand to ensure success. But you also need to understand your context, your own predispositions and be able to adapt to them to suit your situation, both in terms of what you need to do and how you do it.

Figure 1: The giraffe concept

Of course, the giraffe concept doesn't just apply to leadership. It is equally relevant when it comes to teaching strategies, for example. As Dylan Wiliam (2015) argues, 'In education, *what works?* is not really the right question because everything works somewhere and nothing works everywhere. So what's interesting, what's important in education is: *under what conditions does this work?*' School leaders, with their staff, need to use the very best evidence to make sure they are using approaches that suit their context.

So what's the job?

Whether you are running a group of schools or have just taken on your first middle leadership role, the job is basically the same. Pendleton (2012) in his *Primary Colours* model has created an elegant overview of the six key things all leaders need to do. I think it works really well in a school context. It also dovetails with Steve Radcliffe's (2012) simple but brilliantly intuitive leadership framework, Future-Engage-Deliver.

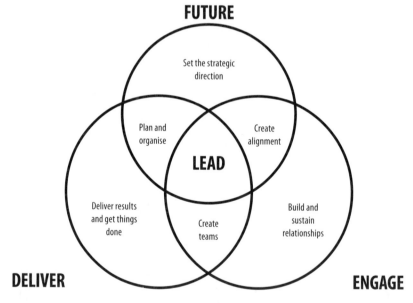

Figure 2: Six key areas for leadership action
Adapted from David Pendleton's Primary Colours model and Steve Radcliffe's Future-Engage-Deliver

This hybrid model can be applied usefully at all levels of leadership and Part 3 of the book takes each element in turn. The first key area focuses on the **future** envisaged for the school as a whole or an individual team. It relates to the shared vision, the approach to managing change and how you make the best use of your resources, both money and people. It's about the extent to which the overall strategy is based on what research and evidence tell you are most effective, and the degree to which you are keen to try out and evaluate new ideas for yourself. For those of you that are system leaders, this is about the strategy underpinning how a group of schools can work together successfully. For a middle leader, it's about translating wider organisational goals into something tangible and ambitious for your frontline team.

Once you are clear on your strategy, the next key area of work is to build and sustain great relationships. Only through the effective **engagement** of others can leaders at any level make change happen. For heads, having a team of staff who are committed to your goals and work well together to support one another in achieving them is at the heart of what makes a great school.

Linked to this is great **delivery**, the third key element in the model. Leadership isn't just about strategy and inspiring others. It's about making sure things happen when you want them to and to the standard you expect. Great schools are the result of great delivery, day-in, day-out. We know that one of the biggest challenges facing schools all over the world is how to create consistent delivery for every pupil, regardless of the curriculum area, their teacher, or their age. The degree of variation of pupil outcomes within schools is still greater than the difference that exists between them.

There are some important inter-plays between these three key leadership areas. It's no good having a great strategy unless you are **planned and organised**. Thinking about how you are properly planned comes more easily to some leaders than others but is critical for us all. No school achieves its full potential if the leaders that are responsible for bringing out the best in pupils and staff are poorly organised. Apart from the obvious confusion and inefficiency that results, the effect on individuals' motivation can also be very detrimental.

You can lead the most harmonious and motivated team but if the individuals in it aren't clear on the shared direction you are headed, you won't achieve the ambitious goals you are striving for. Creating strong **alignment** is therefore critical. Whatever level you are leading at, your staff will be much more effective if everyone is clear on where you are headed and has bought into the vision.

Finally, school leadership at any level is about leading a team of staff, not doing everything yourself. Whilst it can be very tempting to take on tasks, partly because you can usually do the job quicker and better than others, great leaders **create great teams**, delegating tasks and decisions to others. Empowering colleagues in this way, as long as it is done well, has the capacity to significantly increase the quality of delivery overall.

Leadership and management

Distinctions are often made about the difference between leadership and management. Both are critical for the success of a team, school or group of schools. As Peter Drucker (2007) helpfully suggests, "Management is doing things right; leadership is doing the right things." But in schools there are times when the distinction between the two can feel rather artificial. Where, for example, does a good coaching conversation sit? In my view, a coaching conversation is both. You are leading by asking great questions that are helping a colleague to develop and empowering them to lead too. You are managing by engaging in a conversation that is usually about improving delivery, performance and, ultimately, pupil impact.

Which is why David Pendleton's Primary Colours model and Steve Radcliffe's Future-Engage-Deliver models work so well. They both avoid making this distinction whilst at the same time covering the critical elements for each. If leadership is about doing the right things, then there are key elements that relate to strategy. But both also give proper attention to delivery and making things happen, and happen well. And the link between the two is great engagement with those who will make this all happen. This book takes the same approach. However, the emphasis is on providing generic models and guidance that leaders at all levels can apply to their context, rather than providing technical descriptions of more management techniques such as lesson observation.

The way that you lead

Ultimately, the actions that you take as a leader are critical. What you do to create strategy, build relationships and ensure strong delivery will underpin the success of your staff. But it is not as simple as that. Your success as a leader at any level isn't just about what you do. It's also about how you lead, your leadership style and how you support and inspire others to develop. Part 4 of the book discusses the importance for leaders at all levels to (i) build trust, (ii) create a transparency around decision-making and how information is used, (iii) develop the skill of active listening and to develop a critical leadership habit: to *ask first*. These all have the potential to significantly enhance the impact of what you do for all those you work with.

The importance of culture and climate

What you do as a school leader makes a difference to the results you achieve, however you choose to define what you mean by results. But the relationship between leadership and results isn't direct. As the diagram below suggests, the actions you take as a leader have a significant impact on the culture and climate within your sphere of influence.

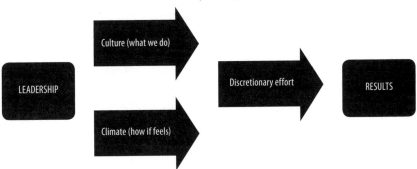

Figure 3: Leadership and results
Adapted from Pendleton and Furnham

In this context, *culture* is taken to mean 'the way we do things around here' and relates to the systems, procedures and common practices and, in particular, to the high standards and expectations that exist in the way these are delivered. A useful way of thinking of culture is to consider what someone new joining your team would see happening on a day-to-day basis and the extent to which everyone in the team is working in the same way and to the same level of expectation. Is there a consistent set of high expectations from you about how your team should work? As a result of this, for example, are the learning environments you oversee inspiring and well organised? Do pupils have strong and supportive relationships with their peers and all the staff they work with?

Climate is more about how it feels to work in a team. For your team, this reflects its morale, how appreciated your team of staff feel and the degree of trust within the team as whole. This is much more difficult to describe or measure, but detailed research has shown that the effect of climate on team productivity is considerable.

Discretionary effort

Taken together, the more positive the culture and climate you create, the more likely your team of staff are to go the extra mile. This concept is known as *discretionary effort*. It is commonly described as the input from individuals over and above that which they need to contribute in order to keep their jobs. Critical in this context, however, is that the effort individuals make is directed productively. You will probably know from your own experience of well-meaning and hard-working colleagues who regrettably did not have the impact that their efforts deserved because they were too often focused on doing the wrong things. In a classroom context, it's all very well having fantastically enjoyable lessons if what the pupils are learning doesn't relate to the curriculum they are meant to be following or the assessments they will have to take!

The diagram below summarises some of the key elements that I believe are most useful in building discretionary effort in schools. Many of these themes are revisited throughout the book. They represent a powerful combination of factors that help to create great schools.

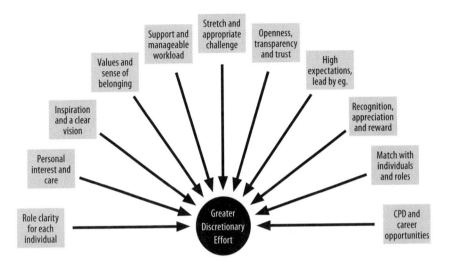

Figure 4: How to build discretionary effort

You would be forgiven for thinking, however, that those with the biggest influence on discretionary effort within a school are members of the senior leadership team. After all, senior leaders surely set the overall ethos for the school? Interestingly, whilst the evidence from a number of studies does show that senior leaders in organisations do have a significant effect on the effort made by staff, the single most influential factor in determining discretionary effort in an individual member of staff is their relationship with and respect for their direct line manager. You only need to go back and look at the list above to realise that for the vast majority of factors, someone's line manager is often the best person to help realise each factor.

As the significant majority of staff, particularly in larger schools, are line managed by middle leaders, it is hardly surprising that most heads and governors acknowledge the critical role they play in the success of any school. Middle leaders often really are the *engine-room* of a school.

As well as building discretionary effort, a productive culture and climate also has a positive effect on staff retention. As Richard Branson says: "Train people well enough so they can leave; treat them well enough so that they don't want to". Given the challenges that never seem to go away when it comes to teacher recruitment in many areas, reducing the requirement to attract new staff by retaining those you already have, makes a great deal of sense.

To sum up

The diagram below sums up the overall leadership framework introduced in this chapter. The framework forms the basis for the structure of the rest of the book.

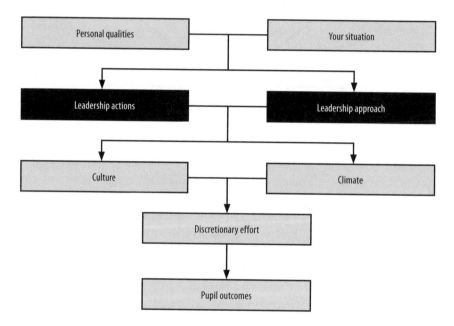

Figure 5: The whole leadership picture

Leadership starts with you. Your understanding of yourself: the way you tend to behave in certain situations, what you enjoy and are good at and those areas you should probably focus on if you want to improve your effectiveness. But you also need to take the time to properly understand your situation: the people and the context you find yourself in.

Taken together, an understanding of self and situation should enable you to decide what the actions are you need to prioritise and the best approach to take in implementing them. If you get this right, you will create a productive culture and climate that combine to release significant discretionary effort from those you lead which will lead to you achieving the pupil outcomes you aspire to.

Using this book

How you access the book is very much up to you. You may wish to dip into chapters as the need arises, or you may wish to work your way through each chapter in order. The book has been structured to work either way. The content has been broken down into manageable chunks. If there is one thing that unites all leaders in schools, it's that there is never enough time, so making the structure as flexible as possible has been an important part of how the book has been organised.

At the end of the book there is a list of the key sources that are referenced in the text.

Part 1

Your personal qualities

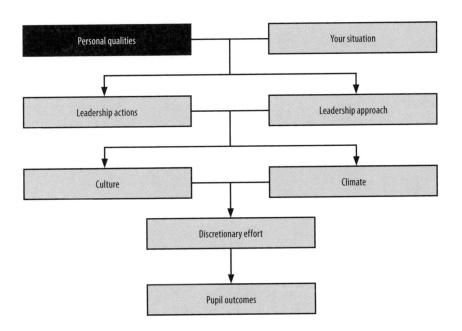

Chapter One

Your leadership predispositions

Predisposition is not predestination.
William Landay

Ever since I can remember, I have read about the importance of leaders knowing themselves. I have to admit that it was only towards the end of my second headship, after more than 15 years in senior leadership roles, that I began to take this sentiment seriously. If I am honest, it always sounded like the sort of thing someone who wasn't actually in a leadership position might say. Something of theoretical interest but of little practical relevance.

As a school leader, what mattered to me was working out the right thing to do and getting everyone doing it to a high standard. So I understood the need to assess a situation. I appreciated the importance of developing strategy. I knew it mattered to get others on board and excited about what we wanted to achieve. I knew it was important to monitor progress and outcomes closely to see how we were doing.

But what I didn't allow for were my own predispositions in all of that. All of us respond to situations in different ways, both emotionally and rationally. We bring all sorts of preconceptions and predispositions to situations. We are more or less able to accurately read the emotions of others or even to manage our own if we are able recognise them. All of which makes us more or less able to make good decisions or form effective relationships with others.

I can recall many situations when, for whatever reason, things didn't always work out the way I had hoped. When I look back on my first headship, my default reaction was usually to blame, not to try to find out why something hadn't worked. This was often followed by trying, usually single-handedly, to find a solution and then pretty much impose it on everyone else. Alongside this, I was quick to make judgements about others' competence. Sometimes people decided it was best to leave the school. Of course, in many cases this was the right thing. Great schools, to use Jim Collins' analogy in Good to Great (2001), are good at getting the right people on the bus and the wrong people off. As a leader at any level, you need to be clear about the standards you expect and hold others to account. But I think I was too quick to act in some of these situations. I am naturally predisposed to take swift and decisive action without always taking the time to think something through. It is a preference I am still working to manage; a habit I am still changing.

So what can the experts tell us about all this? Chapter two on self-awareness looks at two key theories:

1. Ingram and Luft's Johari window (1955)

2. Goleman's emotional intelligence model (2000)

I am not a psychologist. But what I share in chapter 2 are my practical reflections on these models. Why understanding one's own predispositions means, as a school leader, you will be able to make better decisions, manage relationships more effectively and be better placed to ensure great delivery.

Sharing your predispositions with others can also be powerful. If colleagues know the things you are good at and enjoy doing, the whole team can benefit from those strengths. If there are things that energise you, let others know. Conversely, if there are particular behaviours that de-motivate or irritate you, let others know these too. Finally, if there are particular predispositions that you are working to manage more effectively, it can be helpful to let colleagues know. Not only can they give you feedback when you are doing well on these, which is helpful in itself, they can also give a gentle reminder when you are not!

The remaining two chapters in this part of the book focus on key personal qualities that appear to underpin great school leadership at all levels. Chapter 3 examines the importance of personal drive. Chapter 4 reminds us that great leaders show humility. They are very good at their job and achieve great things for the pupils they serve but never forget it is a team effort.

Summary

- Do you know your own predispositions as a leader?
- Do you play to your strengths?
- Are there any areas you know you need to keep in mind and try to manage more effectively as they have the potential to limit your effectiveness?
- How can others help you achieve these?

Chapter Two

Self-awareness

I think self-awareness is probably the most
important thing towards becoming a champion.
Billie Jean King

'Know thyself' was written on the forecourt of the Temple of Apollo at Delphi as a message to the philosophers, statesmen and law-givers who laid the foundation for western culture. It is one of the greatest challenges for every leader: to know their strengths and development areas, to know what arouses strong emotions in themselves and how to manage them.

If you are a middle leader, stepping into a leadership role for the first time, your voyage of self-discovery is usually faster than it will be at any other point in your career. You are learning all the time, taking on new responsibilities, managing up and down, and often still have a pretty full timetable and little time to step back and reflect.

Your experiences and strengths as a teacher helped you reach your middle leadership position, and while you need to retain those strengths in your new role, you are now exposing yourself to new challenges which will create new development areas. This is where senior leaders can really add value. They can help MLs identify their new development areas and support them, through mentoring and coaching, to build their skills in these areas. They can also help them reflect on how they are progressing.

But for more senior leaders, too, the journey to self-awareness never ends. As I mentioned earlier, it took rather too long for me to realise the potential and power of strong self-awareness.

Knowing yourself

There are a number of ways you can get to know yourself better. One way is, of course, to build honest and open relationships so people just say it to you as it is! But this isn't always easy to do, particularly when it comes to getting feedback from people from within your team. One way round this is for you to take part in a more structured 360-feedback survey. There are a number of variations on how a 360 survey can be conducted, but they are basically designed to allow you to reflect on your own strengths and areas for development and then see how they align with the perceptions of around five other colleagues. This feedback will usually come from a range of individuals: those who are more senior than you, your peers and those who are part of your team. In other words, they represent a 360-view.

Whilst these are starting to become a little more commonplace than they were a few years ago, we are a long way from all middle and senior leaders viewing 360 feedback as a routine part of the feedback they should routinely expect to receive to support their development. Part of the reason for this is that it has either been very expensive or time-consuming to operate 360 surveys for all leaders in a school or group of schools. However, there are a number of online options that schools can consider, some of which represent excellent value. At Leadership Matters, we have created our own 360 survey based around the leadership model underpinning this book.

You can also use one of the many personality tools available to increase self-awareness. Some good examples include the Myers-Briggs Type Indicator (MBTI) that can give an indication of behaviour preferences against four opposing dichotomies. At Leadership Matters we have developed an online tool that is also based on a Jungian approach. Crucially, with any of these personality tools, it is important not to use the outcome of any process to help you justify to yourself or others why you can't do certain things. For example, someone who likes leaving things to the last minute and prefers to keep things open and flexible (which can be a strength in itself in certain situations) shouldn't allow this to be a reason why they can't be more planned and organised. Just like writing with your other hand, it is just a bit more difficult and takes more deliberate practice.

These tools will allow you to reflect on your own strengths and development areas, or compare your perceptions against others'. They may confirm what you knew already or, most helpfully, tell you something you didn't know. The Johari window (Luft and Igham, 1955) is a model that groups these areas into four categories:

1. *open*, which are those known by you and others;

2. *hidden*, which are known by you but which you do not reveal to others;

3. *blind spot*, which are those others know about you but you do not know about yourself, and

4. *unknown* which are those that are not known to you or others.

The unknown areas are the hardest to discover and, apart from using 360 feedback, often the best way to find these is when you put yourself in new or particularly challenging situations, when more concealed emotions are often heightened and become more evident.

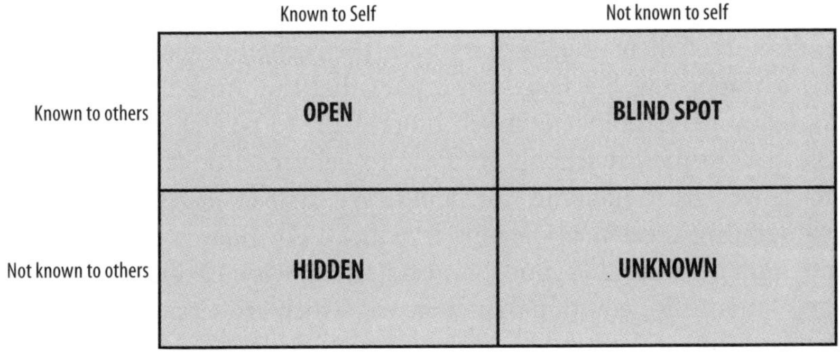

	Known to Self	Not known to self
Known to others	**OPEN**	**BLIND SPOT**
Not known to others	**HIDDEN**	**UNKNOWN**

Figure 6: The Johari window
Luft and Igham

Consistent review

Whatever your leadership role, making time to regularly review your own performance is a useful habit to develop.

There are four ways you can do this:

- Make the time to reflect – do you systematically and regularly make time to think about effectiveness of your leadership practice?
- Ask for feedback – do you make a point of asking for feedback from colleagues, parents, pupils and peers?
- Practise mindfulness – what strategies do you use to relax and create the mental space for you to reflect?
- Have a critical friend – who do you speak to beyond your line manager in order to process their thoughts and ideas and get an external perspective on their challenges? Might you benefit from having a coach, particularly if you are facing an exciting but slightly daunting leadership transition?

Emotional intelligence

The last fifteen years has seen the emergence of the concept of emotional intelligence (EQ). Setting aside the debate about whether this is an intelligence at all, or simply a personal competence, in his seminal article for the Harvard Business Review, *Leadership that gets results* (2000), Daniel Goleman's model brought the idea to international prominence. He suggests that a leader's EQ is likely to be a much more important indicator of their effectiveness than their intelligence (IQ). Of course IQ is important, but Goleman argues that the thing that distinguishes *standout* performance is much more likely to be EQ. This makes a lot of sense to me. In schools we need to deliver through others if we are to deliver great outcomes for pupils. We can't do everything ourselves, so building great relationships is critical. For busy school leaders, the strength of Goleman's model is also its simplicity. He identified just four key domains for emotional intelligence, which are set out in the diagram below.

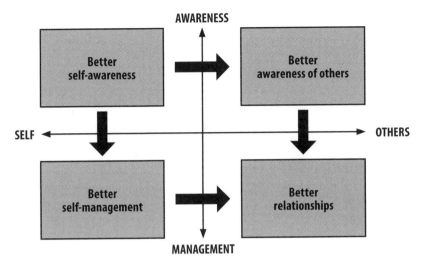

Figure 7: a model of emotional intelligence
Daniel Goleman

As the model summarises, Goleman believes emotional intelligence begins with better self-awareness. This in turn supports one's awareness of others and provides an opportunity for you to manage your own emotions. Together, the combination of these two provides the basis by which one is able to build better relationships. Going right back to the start of this part of the book, it is why self-awareness in leaders matters so much as it pretty much defines one's ability to build relationships with others, which is critical for any leader.

Understanding your emotional responses

Whilst colleagues, parents and pupils might detect external signs of your behaviour in a difficult conversation, none will usually be able to identify how you are feeling inside. A difficult discussion with a parent whose child might require the support of social services, or a member of staff who is not following a departmental or school marking policy will arouse a range of emotions. Similarly, how are you likely to respond if you are told you are going to need to make significant budget cuts or need to make colleagues redundant?

These emotional responses are natural and not a sign of vulnerability. If you can identify these and know what kinds of situations trigger stress or emotional responses in you, then you have a better chance of remaining in control of a situation. Being able to identify situations that arouse strong emotions means you can identify and interpret those emotions. It also allows you to remain more objective. A powerful strategy can be to reflect on a situation by imagining yourself stepping outside your body and viewing your situation objectively. What will you tell yourself to do?

Role-modelling self-awareness

This works at two levels. Ideally, you want to build a culture and climate in your own team where self-awareness is valued and practised. It can be incredibly powerful for your team to see you role model being self-aware or acting as the 'learning-centred leader'. One of the most striking ways to do this is for you to admit that you do not know the answer to something, or that you need the support of your team to solve a problem. This shows others that continuous learning and reflection is nothing to be ashamed of and it is an important part of developing as a leader.

If you are feeling confident, you might even admit a development area or a challenge and invite feedback or ideas from colleagues. In *The Advantage*, Lencioni (2014) describes a range of team exercises that use the sharing of feedback as a mechanism for building trust and establishing a culture of reflection. For example, you might invite your team to give you feedback on how you could have handled a situation differently. By putting yourself in the position of receiving feedback, you powerfully model that you value reflection and self-awareness.

Summary

- Do you use the Johari window to help you see yourself and others more clearly?
- What steps and processes do you go through to regularly review your own self-awareness and their changing leadership style/role?
- How do you model these approaches for other leaders?

Chapter Three

Courage

Anyone can hold the helm when the sea is calm.
Publilius Syrus

Leadership at any level in a school brings with it many challenges. This chapter looks at the importance of having the courage to do the right thing and keep going.

The challenges of middle leadership

If you are a middle leader, your job is undoubtedly one of the most pressurised in school. Whilst senior leaders are in control of whole-school strategy and direction, as a middle leader you sit at the heart of the school leadership team managing up, down and across, implementing the changes that come from above and managing the situations which arise below you. The role of middle leaders is also shifting, demanding more autonomy and accountability, which makes resilience and courage more important than ever before.

Changes from government policies can often mean you are at the heart of implementing regular change coming from outside your school as well. You are faced with more ambiguity, inconsistency and change from above and outside, making long-term decisions harder to reach. Whilst in theory you may have more autonomy, it often doesn't feel like that. Technology has removed physical barriers so you can be reached anywhere, anytime and do not have the time and space to think.

Senior leadership

It might seem obvious, but as a senior leader, whilst the potential impact of your work and decisions you make can be much greater, so too is the potential for pressure and worry. Decisions you take have bigger implications for both you personally if things go wrong, the school, your staff and, most importantly, your pupils. The pressure of public accountability, particularly for heads and system leaders, is significant. As with middle leadership, external pressures are significant. It can sometimes feel like expectations keep rising, finding great teachers gets harder and there is never enough resource to do what you really believe needs to be done.

Added to this is the pressure that comes from dealing with the unplanned events that never fail to arrive at just the wrong time. I remember talking to one head a few years ago who described how she had to lead her school into an inspection in the same week that a member of her staff had committed suicide following a school-related incident. In such circumstances, the best leaders seem to draw on an indescribable source of inspiration and energy that lies deep within their psyche. In this case, the head concerned led her school to its first-ever outstanding judgement.

The unshakeable conviction and determination to do what it takes in order to do the right thing for the school and the young people that it serves seems to be at the heart of the drive and passion that circumstances like this bring forth from these outstanding leaders.

So what is it that great leaders at all levels do that makes a difference?

Managing your emotions

In order to stay strong for your team, you have to stay strong yourself, which means managing your emotions, as we saw in chapter 2. Emotions are not a sign of weakness, in fact recognising and identifying how you are feeling is a real strength. Different situations make different people feel stressed. Do you know what situations make you feel stressed? Do you know what makes you worry or feel anxious? The important thing is to recognise your emotions but not be governed by them.

If you recognise your emotions then you probably know how to manage them. Maybe when you feel stressed or worried you need to talk to someone you trust to get a different perspective. Maybe you need to create some personal space to think through the problem. Maybe you need to go for a run or do something different to clear your head.

Some questions to ask yourself might include:

- How do I feel?
- Why do I feel that way (e.g. recent event, criticism)?
- Is this something that normally triggers an emotional response?
- What would I tell myself to do if I were observing from outside?

Turning negativity into positivity

In the moments of highest pressure and negative criticism you have two choices: you can either let the criticism build into a negative spiral, or you can see and use it as an opportunity to respond positively and build support. If you can soak up the criticism, show you are listening, prove to others that you want to adapt, improve and learn, then you can turn negative situations into positive ones. The game is only over if you give up.

Put yourself in the position of the person giving feedback or criticism. Often they may just want to voice frustration, they may be under pressure themselves that they are projecting, or they may really care and sound negative because they want things to be better. Either way, you cannot lose if you respond positively. If you can tap into why they are behaving the way they are then you can use their feedback to build support.

Some questions you may want to ask:

- How are they behaving (anger, frustration, or commitment)?
- What are they saying (do they want improvement, change, or vindication)?
- What is behind the words (influence, affirmation, or veiled support)?
- What do they want to hear (apology, commitment to change, or that they are right)?

Staying optimistic

If you can manage yourself and not let the external criticism get on top of you, then the next group to focus on is your team. Jon Coles, my former boss at United Learning and a former senior director at the Department for Education, talks about leaders needing to exhibit *unwarranted optimism*. Staff look to leaders in school for reassurance when things are difficult. They need to see leaders being optimistic, however hard this is to do, to make them feel secure in difficult or uncertain circumstances.

Here are some practical ways in which this can be achieved:

- Recognising and celebrating small successes to build momentum and positivity in the team;
- Praising the team to keep them positive – you will also find that makes you more positive too;
- Communicating so that others hear your voice regularly and you control the flow of information and messages;
- Being authentic and honest so they feel they can trust you to deliver the tough message when it's required;
- Copying role models – when you are feeling vulnerable, copy the behaviour of others who appear in control;
- Communicating your vision – your vision will inspire the team and remind them about the big picture reason behind what you are doing.

Learning and improving from criticism

The first thing about criticism is not to try and analyse it in the moment. Often it is hard to be objective about criticism and pressure when you are receiving it because emotions, sensitivities and fears are heightened. If you feel like you want to give feedback or find yourself using language of blame or fault then it may not be the right time to analyse. The heat of the moment is not the time to start saying 'if only we had done this...'

Keep a log of the feedback, problems and actions so that you can look back once the crisis has passed and everyone has found something to be positive about. You are then in a safe space to look back and analyse what has happened. Let everyone share their perspectives and what they would do, finding time and space to listen and digest the different information you are hearing. Make sure that any face-to-face conversations are held in private and not in public if you need to have tough conversations.

Finally, make sure everyone commits to the changes you want to make. Allowing them to feed in will be critical, but make sure they know you are still committed, motivated and positive that the team can succeed moving forward.

Keeping going

Peter Matthews in his Ofsted publication, *Twelve outstanding secondary schools (2009)* talks about the 'tireless energy' that leaders in the schools he studied demonstrated. Their schools didn't become outstanding overnight. It was the culmination of hard work over a significant period of time. The building of this momentum is the culmination of an ongoing determination and rigorous focus on a school's core business. For school leaders, the implication is very clear: running a successful school takes a huge amount of hard work! Not just because it is important that school leaders need to be seen to be leading by example, but also because there appears to be almost no other way. Just when you have one thing sorted, something else crops up. There is always something else to do...

None of the heads I have met in the last few years give the impression that their workload had diminished in any way. In fact the reverse is probably true.

Taking calculated risks

The last area this chapter relates to is the importance of school leaders taking risks. This takes courage in itself. Not that these risks won't have been carefully considered before they are taken. To take one example, giving relatively junior members of staff key roles within a school can easily backfire. Yet this approach can have a major impact in helping create a culture where people learn on the job and develop themselves, becoming self-motivated and self-disciplined. It also provides a clear sense that the leadership of the school values the people that work there, which builds a positive climate. Together, taking these risks and having the courage to believe in colleagues builds momentum, leadership capacity, and enhances trust.

The very best leaders also have the courage to take risks about what they are *not* to going to do. Jim Collins' *hedgehog concept* is all about keeping the focus on what an institution knows it does well and is its core business. Deciding not to undertake certain activities, even when all around them are, takes courage. I remember as a head, a few years ago now, when we decided our school would not engage with the new Diploma qualification. We just weren't convinced it was going to work in practice. This was most definitely a risky strategy, as government had set a date when all schools needed to provide their pupils access to the range of Diploma qualifications. But it was a calculated risk and one based upon doing what we thought was right for our pupils. In the end, the qualification wasn't popular with pupils, parents and schools nationwide and the initiative folded.

The excellent NCSL (2004) publication 'A model of urban leadership in challenging urban environments' describes how the best leaders show courage by:

1. standing up for their beliefs and defending them in the face of opposition and entrenched interests;

2. doing the right thing rather than taking the easy option, despite the possible risks and complications;

3. taking calculated risks, where appropriate, to improve provision for students.

One head once told me how his school had decided to create a two-year KS3 well before anyone else had done this. Yet four years later, with the abolition of KS3 SATs, many schools decided to follow suit. The same school also decided to do away with tutor groups and tutorial time in favour of dedicated one-to-one coaching for students provided by all the adults working at the school. For this trailblazing school, both decisions were calculated risks that took courage, but both ultimately contributed to the school gaining its first outstanding judgement that year.

One leader of a multi-academy trust I know decided with senior colleagues a few years ago that they would only take new schools into their trust if they were within a close geographical area, to allow for meaningful collaboration and the flexible deployment of staff. At that time, government policy was to grow the academies movement as fast as possible, and the trust was risking losing government support for its stance. In the end, however, time has shown this approach to growth to have been a successful strategy and indeed government policy has changed to reflect this.

Having courage comes from both self-confidence and an inner strength, often derived from a strong sense of moral purpose combined with innate self-belief. In the leaders of our most successful schools, at all levels, there is ample evidence of both.

Key points

- How good are you at appreciating and managing your emotions?
- Are you able to keep optimistic, even in the most difficult circumstances?
- Do you usually learn from your mistakes?
- Are you good at taking those difficult decisions or occasionally admitting publicly when you are wrong?
- Do you have the courage to take calculated risks, even if this sometimes involves going out on a limb?

Chapter Four

Humility

Humility is not thinking less of yourself;
it's thinking of yourself less.

C. S. Lewis

When thinking about the structure of this book, it was tempting to include the contents of this short chapter in with one of the others. However, whilst this part of the book makes a simple point that doesn't take a huge amount of explaining, to have included it as part of another chapter would have undermined its importance.

When Jim Collins in his book *Good to Great* (2001), looked at the companies that he judged had made the move from good to great, he discovered something very interesting about the leaders of those companies. Unsurprisingly, all of them were very ambitious. However, this ambition was not focused on their own achievements but on being ambitious for their organisation. They were, in fact, very modest about their own personal achievements. When they talked about their companies, it was more as if their successes were as a result of a huge team effort of which they had the privilege to be at the helm.

The power of humility

When I was responsible for running the London Challenge *Good to Great* programme, as the head of a school that was judged 'good' at the time, we used to invite heads from schools that had been judged outstanding three or four times to come and talk to us about their journeys. As we listened to these successful school leaders at our conferences, exactly the same phenomenon that Jim Collins identified emerged strongly. The heads all extolled the virtues of their staff, pupils and the support they had received from the families in their community. Of course, they acknowledged the importance of their own personal leadership and their drive for continuous improvement. But they were all modest about their achievements, wanting always to give the credit to others rather than to themselves.

But in some ways, this finding isn't that surprising. After all, this is exactly the type of leadership that will build trust amongst staff and help people to develop themselves and learn in the workplace. It will also encourage an open, honest and transparent environment where leaders have the emotional intelligence and self-awareness to recognise the importance of celebrating the achievements of everyone, whilst at the same time keeping the focus on performance and continuous improvement.

But the definition of humility here is not about false modesty. These leaders have a grounded and honest sense of who has achieved what. They are confident about their own abilities and don't need to prove themselves to others by advertising their own achievements.

Respecting uncertainty

But as Michael Fullan (2008) points out in *The six secrets of change*, there is another reason why effective leaders remain humble. Schools are no different from any other organisation in that they operate within an incredibly complex environment. For example, how we should use new technologies such as social networking to support learning, what we know about how the brain works, the challenges of recruiting teachers and the rapid changes to population demographics all present leaders of our schools with an ever-changing landscape.

Any leader who is not humbled by the complexities of such an environment and who doesn't recognise the need to keep learning and keep up to speed with the developments around them is unlikely to remain as a leader in a high performing school.

Building momentum, loyalty and trust

There is also clear evidence that leaders who don't see themselves as being above certain types of work have a strong impact on building momentum. Peter Matthews (2009) was clear in his study of *Twelve outstanding schools* that the heads and other school leaders, however senior, all recognised the importance of being 'hands on'. The school leaders who are prepared to demonstrate that they have both the ability and willingness to tackle the tasks that they expect everyone else to do not only gain huge personal respect but help create the kind of alignment that builds organisational momentum.

This is humility in a different sense. It is making a clear statement that a leader is no better than anyone else. That they understand they are part of a team where everyone is an essential part of that team and where the individual role that each person plays is critical to the success of the whole school.

Demonstrating the willingness to carry out any role also builds trust, particularly when taking the time to join with others in what might be seen as more menial tasks such as putting out the chairs for assembly, serving school lunches when they are short staffed or signing in parents at a parents' evening. Where such action is linked with small acts of kindness, they are even more powerful. For example, when a leader offers to do duty or take a register for a colleague who just needs some time alone for a moment, the loyalty that that simple act buys will inevitably be multiplied ten times over.

A focus on the school, not the leader

In drawing this chapter to a close, it is important to remember that I am not saying the best leaders are not ambitious, competitive or driven. They are absolutely focused on achieving the best they can for their teams and their schools. What sets the leaders in the best schools apart is that the ambition is for the school itself, not for them as an individual.

This links back to the importance of moral purpose I discussed earlier. The most successful leaders want the best for their pupils. Of course, it is important that their work is enjoyable, fun and personally rewarding. But the main motivator is the success of the organisation as a whole, not for them as an individual leader.

Key points

- Do you give credit to others for the success of your team or school(s)?

- Are you emotionally self-aware? If yes, how do you know?!

- Are you prepared to lead by example in any role in order to portray yourself as not being too important to do certain types of work?

- Are you always keen to learn more and keep improving?

Part 2

Your situation

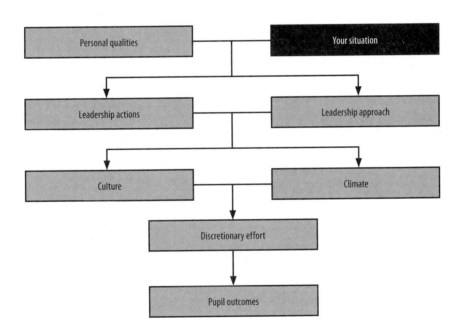

Chapter Five

Those around you

> It is not easy in this world for one person
> to understand the next one.
> Goethe

Part one of this book was about the importance of taking time to properly understand your own predispositions and proactively take steps to play to your strengths as well as manage both your emotions and your habits in those areas that might reduce your effectiveness as a leader. You may remember this was something, with hindsight, that I think I appreciated rather late in my own development as a leader!

This next part of the book is all about the other half of this equation. Not your internal world that has been our focus so far, but the external world within which you lead. This could be a part of your school, the whole school or even a group of schools, depending on your role. But crucially, before you decide what you need to focus on as a leader, or how you might go about implementing these priorities, you need to understand your situation properly.

At the highest level, this breaks down into two key areas. Firstly, how well developed is your area of responsibility or the school you lead? Where are you on your journey? The next chapter looks at this in more detail. The focus of this chapter, however, is on your understanding of the people you are working with. Just like you, they will have their own predispositions, strengths and areas for development. But do you know what they are? And do you consciously and deliberately think about your approach with individuals you interact with and reflect those differences? Or do you just tend to work with everyone the same way, perhaps more reflecting your own preferences than what is going to get the best out of them?

Getting to know others

Many of the suggestions in the earlier chapters about how you can get to know yourself apply equally when thinking about others. Using personality tools and 360 surveys can be helpful. So too, can using data effectively to monitor outcomes and performance, more of which in the next chapter.

But there is also huge potential to understand colleagues from your day-to-day interactions with them, whether you are a middle leader, senior leader or running a school or group of schools. Whatever your circumstances, there will be key people with whom you work that it will be useful for you to know and understand well, including those that report to you, your peers and others who may be more senior than you (including governors and trustees). So how do you make the most of these interactions?

At its heart, your approach needs to focus on taking the time and effort to listen to and observe colleagues carefully. Whilst the quote from Mehrabian (1972) that, in essence, says 'only 7% of communication comes from what is said; whereas 38% is through tone of voice and 55% from reading body language' is often taken out of its original context, it is a helpful reminder that we need to be attuned to all three of these aspects of communication. It can also be really useful to develop a habit that the final chapter of this book will explore in much more detail: that of *asking first*. By asking neutral questions, you can establish much more quickly where someone is with their thinking or level of motivation on an issue.

What are you looking for?

In simple terms, leaders need to try to understand others' competence, preferred ways of working and their motivations. If you are able to work these out, you are in a position to tailor your approach accordingly. Let's say you are introducing a new idea. Some of your colleagues may be keen to properly understand how this idea fits into the wider strategy before getting into the detail. Others, on the other hand, need to understand the detail of how something is going to work in practice before they are interested in its place within the wider strategy. If you were to pitch a new idea to an individual and didn't factor these preferences into your explanation, you will inevitably create reduced buy-in or engagement for the project from those individuals.

Similarly, some of your team will be much happier if you have a clear implementation plan already mapped out so they can clearly see that the way ahead is organised and decided. For others, this matters much less. In fact, some colleagues may rather not have too much tied down too soon, as this may limit your flexibility to amend your approach as you go.

Playing to strengths

One other key reason for getting to know your team well is to find out what they are good at and make sure you and colleagues take the opportunity to play to their strengths. In her great article, *The incomplete leader*, Deborah Ancona (2007) argues that the very best leaders know what it is they are good at and find other people to lead on the areas they are not. Apart from this making sense at the most basic level, it is also an approach that builds individuals' level of motivation for two reasons: firstly, because you or a colleague have identified their strength in the first place; and secondly, because we all like doing things we are good at. So from every perspective, as well as making sure you not only have the right people on the bus, as Jim Collins (2001) would say, you also need to make sure everyone is in the right seat.

Managing differential performance in others

As well as knowing about how others prefer to work and playing to their strengths, the very best leaders in schools, at all levels, are good at knowing how well colleagues in their team are performing and respond accordingly. Pendleton and Furnham (2012) have developed an interesting model (see below) which suggests leaders can group colleagues according to the behaviours and values of others and their performance at work.

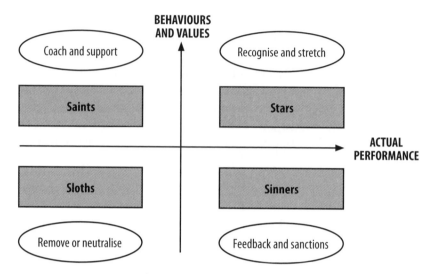

Figure 8: Performance and behaviours
Adapted from Pendleton and Furnham

Let's begin with the stars. These are your high performers who are doing a great job and work in a way that is absolutely in line with the culture and climate you wish to create. They are also the group you need to be careful not to overlook or take for granted. Just like you, they need to be challenged, stretched and recognised for what they do. The more they feel they have a say in their future, the better, but you need to make sure you don't over promise. They will usually appreciate development opportunities, whether formal or informal. They may also be useful when it comes to coaching others, in particular your saints.

At the other extreme are your sloths. These are individuals who are performing poorly and are potentially having a pernicious effect on your culture and climate. You need to quickly understand what sits behind their poor outcomes and attitude and give them very clear and unambiguous feedback about what needs to change in relation to both. Make it clear they are making choices about their future. They then need to improve very quickly or there will be consequences. Ultimately, and with dignity, you need to be prepared to work out a way for them to leave fast.

Your saints are very well-meaning members of your team but they are just not very good. As with the sloths, you need to take time to understand what is stopping them from doing a good job and then make sure they are supported and coached to improve. So long as they continue to improve at a sufficient rate, you should continue to support them. Only if they seem to have peaked at a point that is below your expectations should you consider how they might also move on to pastures new.

Finally, the toughest group of all are your sinners! These are high performing individuals who get great results and achieve strongly. But they do it in a way that undermines the culture and climate you are trying to establish. They don't, for example, get reports written on time nor follow behaviour systems properly. They are often disloyal about your leadership and others in the wider team. In short, they are an annoying thorn in your side. If you have inherited a team whose performance across the board is poor, you may decide you have to live with your sinner(s) for a while – just having anyone who is performing is the priority. But if, over time, it feels like you have reached a tipping point where their negative effect on the wider team is exceeding the positive impact of their own performance, action to address their shortcomings is probably needed. Unlike the saints, who need coaching, what they need is to be given very clear feedback about what needs to change and by when. Coaching probably isn't what's needed. They just need to decide to change or to face the consequences. Ultimately they may need to leave too, if changes don't occur.

Most schools are better at dealing with saints than sinners, partly as there is usually much more written down about the levels of competence that need to be achieved. But having clear statements of expectations around behaviours expected is equally important if one is to tackle what, for sinners, are more likely to be disciplinary issues than those relating to competence.

I don't think Pendleton and Furnham are suggesting you should put each of your staff into one of the boxes and label them in this rather 'black and white' way. People are usually more complex than this. But the model does provide a useful way for you to think about how different individuals may need different approaches that are centred on them rather than the way you tend to respond to any situation, regardless of context.

Key points

- Do you understand others' personality predispositions? Do you use any personality tools to support this?
- Do you use 360 reviews or other mechanisms to better understand the performance of others around you?
- How good are you at really focussing on what others are saying or what their tone of voice and body-language is telling you?
- How well do you deliberately play to others' strengths?
- How good are you at consciously differentiating the way you work with colleagues who display different behaviours or levels of performance?

Chapter Six

Your context

A few observations and much reasoning lead to error;
many observations and a little reasoning to truth.
Alexis Carrel

Understanding your context properly is crucial before deciding upon your priorities for action and approach to implementation. The last chapter focused on knowing the people around you; their strengths, weaknesses and predispositions. This chapter looks at context in a broader sense. How well do you know your operating context, whether that is a curriculum or pastoral area within a school, a school itself or a group of schools? Working out your strategy has to begin with where you are and what you need to do to get to where you want to go.

Performance data can tell you a lot about your context, particularly when the data is benchmarked against similar schools and national averages. But there are many other sources of evidence that you may want to take into account, as performance data alone can sometimes present quite a narrow snapshot of context.

Many schools use anonymous survey or questionnaire data to identify strengths and areas for development. The majority of the tools available provide useful data on national averages that enable you to benchmark your current position. At Leadership Matters, we have developed three simple online survey tools that provide powerful feedback from three key stakeholder groups: pupils, parents and staff. The latter, of course, gives you a great insight into how levels of discretionary effort are improving over time.

But there is also no substitute for talking to as many people as you can, at every opportunity, and in a way that means that people feel at ease to say what they really think, which is a skill in itself! Apart from gleaning useful information, spending time talking to colleagues can do a lot to increase engagement and discretionary effort, so long as people feel that it has been a genuine process. I know a number of heads that interviewed every single member of staff when they joined their school to find out what was working well and what would make the school even better. The impact on staff was universally important – everyone likes to feel they have been heard. I even know one head who, after more than 15 years' headship in the same school, still meets with every member of the teaching and support staff every single year!

Knowing what is going on

More formal monitoring within a school enables you, at any point in time, to know where things are. It's how you really do know the deal that your pupils are getting. It is a way of properly understanding your culture.

There are a number of approaches to monitoring that you can implement and the more you link them together, the more accurate your monitoring will be.

Learning walks give you an idea of where every class and teacher is in terms of teaching and learning and the learning environment. They tend to fall on a spectrum: they can be extremely formal (e.g. 10 minute observations with written feedback); focused (e.g. a weekly or daily focus on marking, differentiation, assessment for learning); or a 'pop in' (which would involve an interaction with the teacher, interaction with some or most of the pupils and gauging the quality of teaching and learning). No doubt your school will have developed a set of working practices.

However this is practically organised in your school, there are some key fundamentals about monitoring:

1. Everyone involved needs to accept the approach and buy in to the idea of how it is being done.

2. You need to ensure that everyone knows exactly why monitoring is so important and that the outcome will contribute to the raising of standards.

3. There should be guidelines for the way in which learning walks will be done.

4. Finally, what and how will the feedback occur? What can people expect in the form of feedback, how often will it be and what will they be expected to do with it?

You and your colleagues need to stick to these so that you deliver a consistent, fair and helpful monitoring process.

Work scrutinies are exactly the same. Marking and planning should be reviewed regularly. Again, clear expectations that are communicated clearly help everyone and ensure good buy-in. You might want to create a calendar of scrutinies at the start of the year and an organised pro-forma of what to expect in terms of when and what the feedback will be to help embed open, transparent and systematic self-evaluation. In addition, why not build up an abundance of excellent practice which when modelled and shared will help everyone to know where the bar has been set and to celebrate good practice? If the climate of learning walks is one of recognition and reward rather than of fear and blame, underpinned with a set of basic expectations, their power to support teacher development is significant.

Combining your evidence

As you will be well aware, the more you can triangulate your evidence, the more accurate the picture you can create of where you are on your journey. Using pupil progress data, broken down to pupil sub-groups, phases or curriculum areas and linking this to other evidence from lesson observations, learning walks and pupil voice, you can start to gain a much more reliable notion of the key measure we all care about most: the impact of teaching over time. We all know the teachers that can turn on a good lesson when they are being observed. But it is highly debatable whether that gives an indication of typicality of teaching or, when combined with quality of feedback, the typicality of pupil progress. And even if it did, Michael Strong's (2011) work on lesson observation calls into question the reliability of grading single lessons in this way anyway.

		Probability that 2nd rater disagrees	
1st rater gives	**%**	**Best case** $r = 0.7$	**Worst case** $r = 0.24$
Outstanding	12%	51%	78%
Good	55%	31%	43%
Req. Impr.	29%	46%	64%
Inadequate	4%	62%	90%
Overall		**39%**	**55%**

Percentages based on simulations

Figure 9: Reliability of lesson observations

Adapted by Rob Coe based on the work of Michael Strong (2003)

As the table above shows, there is a significant chance that two observations of the same lesson can reach a different conclusion as to the overall lesson grade.

So as well as understanding those around you, it is also critical to be clear about your wider context, taking into account as many sources of data and information as you can. Whatever level of leadership you are operating at, this will enable you to be even more effective at deciding what you need to do and how to go about doing it.

Summary

- Do you or colleagues use anonymous survey data from pupils, parents and staff to regularly assess the culture and climate?

- How do you monitor the work of your staff and their performance? Are the systems you have established at a whole-school level being robustly and transparently implemented?

- Do your staff understand why observation and monitoring is important and have they bought in?

- What are senior leaders doing to moderate and validate the judgements that are being made?

Part 3

Your leadership actions

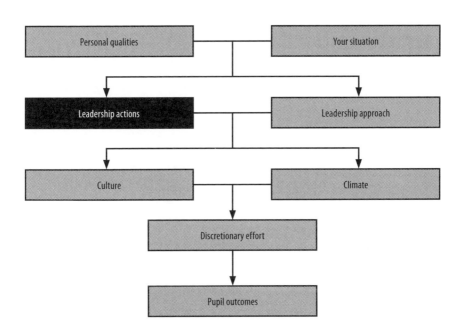

Chapter Seven

Strategy, vision and values

The best CEOs I know are teachers, and at
the core of what they teach is strategy.
Michael Porter

When we heard from heads of schools that had been judged outstanding three or four times at the G2G conferences I ran, a striking feature that regularly emerged was the importance of clarity. Clarity of vision and clarity of strategy. The heads talked about the importance of a clear vision and shared a common purpose as well as, equally importantly, having clarity around the detail of how systems and procedures work in schools: the strategy for achieving them.

In this chapter we shall look at both these areas and draw upon themes from the schools' presentations in addition to some of the points made in Jim Collins' (2001) *Good to Great* in considering what he describes as his *hedgehog concept* as well as examining some of the evidence from Peter Matthews' (2009) Ofsted publication.

We shall also consider the important role that good governance plays in supporting the development of the right strategic approach, drawing on the excellent publication, *A Framework for Governance,* published by the National Governors' Association (2015).

Clarity of goals

All successful schools have a clearly stated set of goals. Everyone involved in a school needs to understand what's expected of them and what the school wants to achieve for all its pupils. But often those goals can be so generic as to be pretty meaningless. The trick is to create goals which carefully define what the distinctive features of the school are, the things that distinguish them from the school down the road.

So how do schools go about arriving at their vision? From an individual perspective, experiences both as a child and as an adult will have shaped the view of what an ideal school should look like, how it should feel and, importantly, how it might work. Almost unconsciously, school leaders and governors know what they want to achieve. However, translating these aspirations into a form of words can be far from easy.

There is also the question of how much the vision of a school should only reflect the views of the head, leadership team or the governing body. There is no doubt that the more people are involved in the process of defining a school's vision, including students themselves, their parents, other school leaders and the staff, the greater the sense of ownership and buy-in.

A shared sense of direction is vital in any school's success. However, consultation of this kind comes with a strong health warning and needs skilful handling by school leaders. The last thing one wants to end up with is a series of bland statements that could apply to any school, which everyone agrees with, but which don't really say anything distinctive.

This challenge is magnified in the context of a group of schools. If you are system leader, you will no doubt recognise the tension between allowing each school its own identity and ensuring that your group of schools can define its distinctive qualities. One way to square this circle, which draws on the giraffe concept in a way, is for a group of schools to define together its key principles (the long neck issues) and then allow each school to interpret and refine these in their own particular context (the markings).

Jim Collins is clear about the importance of organisations really narrowing down the focus of what they are trying to achieve and specifying how they will go about achieving it. To keep the animal analogies going for a moment, he calls this his *hedgehog concept,* based upon the parable of the hedgehog and the fox. Every day the fox tries to outwit the hedgehog, trying a range of different strategies to beat him. What does the hedgehog do? The same thing every time: it rolls up into a prickly ball with success guaranteed on every occasion. The school that jumps on the bandwagon every time a new initiative comes out or the head gets a bright idea is the school that may be good but is unlikely to be consistently outstanding.

Devising strategy

In its excellent publication, *A Framework for Governance* (2015) the National Governors' Association identifies three key objectives for any governing board, whether they have oversight as governors of a single school or as trustees with responsibility of a group of schools:

- Setting the strategic direction;
- Holding the headteacher to account for the educational performance of the school;
- Ensuring financial health, probity and value for money.

The first of these squarely puts strategy at the heart of governance. The role of governors or trustees is to ensure a school has a long-term strategy based on a clear shared vision. Making sure there is also clarity on where the boundary between strategic input and operational delivery sits is also critical. The diagram below summarises how this should work in practice.

Figure 10: Setting the strategy – the role of governance

Adapted from *A Framework for Governance*, National Governors' Association (2015)

The NGA recommend the vision should:

• be ambitious but achievable

• take into account the school's current context

• take account of stakeholders' views

• be agreed and owned by the board

Monitoring delivery

A great strategy without great delivery is a waste of time. As Winston Churchill reminds us: "However beautiful the strategy, one should occasionally look at the results". School leaders and governors need to have robust systems in place to ensure the strategy is being implemented and know the impact on outcomes for pupils. Ensuring objectives are SMART (specific, measurable, achievable, relevant and time-bound) is important. Developing a set of key performance indicators (KPIs) allows this monitoring to focus on the key elements of the strategy. This needs to happen as part of a regular cycle of review.

There also needs to be robust triangulation and verification of the data and information that comes to both senior leaders and governors. Too often where a school is failing, the picture painted all seems fine and then it turns out it wasn't. Governors need to be confident that the picture being painted for them is a real one. Critically, this is about governors and trustees really knowing their schools and, as a result, being able to ask great questions that challenge and properly hold to account as well as recognise and celebrate success.

Objective – strategy – tactics

In his book *Winners*, Alistair Campbell, the former director of communications for Tony Blair, talks about the importance of using *OST*: objective – strategy – tactics. His main point is that once you have an objective, it is really important to consider what your main *single* strategy is for achieving it. He reflects back on the 1997 UK election. Their objective: for Labour to win the election. The strategy: we are *New* Labour. The tactics: a whole series of actions and policies that fitted the overall strategy, such as the removal of Clause 4, making friends with the right-wing press (Rupert Murdoch, in particular) and a new party logo. Outcome: they won the election. Contrast this with Labour's approach to the last election and I can see how there wasn't really an overall game plan. Yes the objective was clear: regain power. But the tactics didn't add up to a coherent strategy. In fact, some of the policies and messaging seemed contradictory. For example, the party was at pains to point out that Labour 'is a friend of business' and 'the economy is safe with us'. Yet at the same time, they were advocating a cap on both energy prices and rents in private sector housing. Of course, hindsight is a wonderful thing, but whatever one's political standpoint, the analysis does resonate. The table below/overleaf takes the approach and applies it in a school context.

Objectives (ideally just 2 or 3 in any given year; maximum of 6; need to be SMART)
• Increase the number of pupils getting to university to 160 by 2022
Strategy (only one for each objective)
• Building independence and a growth mindset
Tactics (linked to each strategy – keep as simple as possible)
• Praise effort and process • Stop using extrinsic rewards such as Vivo points • Organise university trips in Years 7, 9 and 12 • Bring successful former pupils back in Yrs 8, 10, 11 and 13 to inspire pupils • Develop extended project approach from Y7, embedded x-curricular • Provide wide co-curricular opportunities, including sports, arts, travel, adventure, debating, volunteering/volunteering, camps • Organise inspirational visiting speakers who grew up locally

Figure 11: Using OST
Adapted from Alistair Campbell in *Winners*

The critical point here is that, for any given objective, you should ideally aim for only one overall strategy and then line up your tactics underneath this.

In my view, the most successful schools are those that work out a successful strategy and keep to it, making sure that that is what happens day in day out. Having a clarity around core purpose is essential, however simply expressed and however it is arrived at. Even the few words that make up the average school's motto can speak volumes, providing something around which all those who are connected with the school can unite.

As an example, one school I have worked with recently has developed very clear and simple guidelines for all aspects of the school day. There are three key statements that underpin all that the school does and can be applied to any situation by staff or students: 'the street stops at the gate', 'a relentless focus on high standards' and 'there are no barriers or excuses to great learning or achievement'.

Without this clear sense of where a school is meant to be going, there is a strong likelihood that it simply goes nowhere. Staff, students and parents cannot operate with hundreds of policies circulating around their brains. They need clarity around a series of key principles that underpin the way things are expected to happen and where the next time they are not sure about something they can refer back to their understanding of these principles and apply them appropriately. The chances are they will be following policy, so long as policy itself is consistent with the core values and agreed shared ways of working.

The same applies to school leadership at all levels. When decisions need to be made by leaders in school there is nothing more helpful than clear guidance, a clear steer, about how decisions should be made. It is this clarity that breeds trust and confidence from everyone within a school community. It is also what gives senior and middle leaders the platform upon which to make decisions within their own sphere of influence, knowing they will be in line with the overall strategic approach but nuanced by their own circumstances. In other words, once again, the *giraffe concept* in action!

When I reflect back to my time in school, there are a number of areas where I think clarity of purpose is particularly important. Some of these are covered elsewhere in this book, but two deserve further exploration in this chapter. The first is teaching and learning, which should be at the heart of the work of any school. The second is clarity on systems around behaviour and climate for learning.

Clarity of pedagogy

What the most successful schools have done is make sure that every child has a teaching experience that promotes the best possible learning outcomes right across the curriculum, regardless of which teacher they have. They have also managed, by and large, to ensure the job of the teacher is manageable. To achieve this, schools have often undertaken an internal debate: should our school have an overall pedagogical framework?

The answer to this question is not easy. The first part of the debate centres on whether it is desirable to have a shared whole-school approach to pedagogy in the first place. Some would argue that teachers should be free to develop their own approaches to teaching. After all, most teachers have their preferred default teaching methods which probably reflect how they were taught themselves, their initial teacher training and possibly their own preferred way of learning (which often leads to an unconscious tendency to assume that others learn in the same way). Shouldn't the teacher be allowed to concentrate on these areas of strength? By allowing teachers the professional freedom to plan and deliver lessons in their own way, the assumption is that the quality of teaching and learning will be higher.

This may be true to a certain extent, but many successful schools have recognised a number of problems with this approach. Firstly, the quality of planning and resourcing that one teacher can bring to the range of classes they teach is a limiting factor in itself, particularly if there is an expectation that they are supposed to be putting in place an individualised programme in order to meet the needs of each student. Put simply, the task is unmanageable. There are just too many classes, and too much planning and preparation necessary to create the outstanding lessons needed on a consistent basis. This individualised approach also ignores the fact that there may be ways to teach particular skills or knowledge sets that may not be reflected in the individual teacher's repertoire or own experience. In these circumstances there are two possible outcomes: either teachers feel overworked, disenchanted and leave the profession, or they start to cut corners in the name of self-preservation. Clearly, neither of these outcomes is desirable, and certainly hasn't led to the creation of the great schools this publication is about.

What these schools have done is recognise that it makes much more sense for teachers to work together collaboratively to produce high-quality schemes of work for everyone to use. This planning also needs to take a realistic and evidence-based approach to meeting individual student need. Not only does this bring obvious benefits in terms of sharing the workload, it means the quality of teaching and learning will be based on lessons that are planned around a shared view of the best way to teach something. It also provides for the opportunity for those teachers to meet after something has been delivered, share their reflections on what went well and what didn't and make alterations next time around.

To make this shared planning most effective, the best schools have developed a clear view of what makes good teaching itself. This again presents schools with a major challenge. Any teacher will tell you how fast prevailing pedagogical fashions can change. For example, the debate between child-centred or whole-class teaching is always on the agenda, as is the skills versus knowledge debate. In my view, these are often false dichotomies. Great teaching will involve both great explanation and modelling by teachers who have great subject and curriculum knowledge, as well as opportunities for pupils to deepen their understanding and be able to recall what they have learnt in a sophisticated and meaningful way.

Then there are practical considerations, particularly as we know teacher retention will always be a key issue. The most successful schools have recognised that teachers are not superhuman. The leaders of the very best schools do all they can to make the teacher's job as manageable as possible, recognising time constraints and practical classroom issues. But at the same time they make sure that what is created gives teachers the best chance to meet the needs of all their students. As a result, some schools have now set out their broad approach to pedagogy very clearly. Doing so has provided these schools with the opportunity to frame planning around a shared approach that is flexible enough to meet the needs of all the students, play to individual teachers' strengths and allow the different approaches that the range of subjects need. This approach has been about creating a framework, not a straitjacket. It provides a pedagogical bedrock upon which pupil and teacher creativity, experimentation and individuality can thrive.

For example, some schools I have worked with recently have highly developed policy and practice on assessment for learning that has originated from the seminal work of Dylan Wiliam and Paul Black (1998). Another had focused on the importance of developing learning through quality dialogue as described by Robin Alexander (2004) from the University of Cambridge in his work on dialogic teaching. One school has developed a simple summary of what a good lesson looks like. In another, where consistently delivered high quality teaching is at the heart of its approach, every classroom has the teaching framework on the wall. Both staff and students know and understand what is expected. This helps ensure clarity and consistency from all.

Whatever the origins, the benefits provided for both staff and students in schools that have a shared pedagogical approach cannot be underestimated. Not only do teachers have the security of knowing they are working in a collaborative way with their colleagues, even those in other subject disciplines, but students too can benefit from developing their own sense of how they fit into the pedagogical approaches as individual learners. As we will see in later chapters, priority given to developing staff and students is a key feature of the most successful schools. The clarity that a shared pedagogy can bring can be of great benefit in helping to achieve these goals.

Clarity that creates a positive climate for learning

The second area that this chapter will focus on is around how great schools achieve clarity about the way all staff ought to work together with the pupils to promote a consistent approach to management of behaviour and the creation of a positive climate for learning. In his Ofsted publication, Peter Matthews (2009) describes how the outstanding schools he studied had all developed highly effective behaviour policies and were all absolutely clear about the importance of never assuming for one minute that the job of maintaining the right climate for learning is ever finished.

In the very best schools, the equation is simple: in schools with good behaviour, pupils learn more effectively. As well as the obvious direct link between attitudes to learning and learning outcomes, there is another very important factor to consider. The recruitment and retention of good staff is absolutely essential. Schools where staff spend too much of their day trying to maintain discipline are not as effective in attracting and keeping the best teachers and support staff. If good staff leave, then the school can soon find itself on the reverse journey away from its intended destination.

In the most successful schools, all staff play a role in promoting and maintaining a positive learning environment, where good behaviour is encouraged and rewarded and poor behaviour is appropriately punished. In the best schools, effective behaviour management is underpinned by clarity, clear systems and shared understanding.

The biggest challenge for school leaders lies in the process through which one translates these aspirations into the reality of daily life in a school. In great schools a clear message has emerged time and time again: make sure your behaviour policy focuses upon pupils accepting responsibility for their own behaviour and learning. Support your pupils to develop their own self-discipline based upon mutual respect, supported by clear boundaries that are consistently enforced.

Creating a sense within a school of a shared purpose is, as we have already mentioned, very important. Staff, pupils and parents need to have a clear idea about what your school is trying to achieve and why. Of course a well-developed pedagogy is an important part of the equation. If the lessons are interesting, well-paced and meet the pupils' needs, then they are far more likely to respond appropriately. However, there are times when the maintenance of a positive climate for learning sometimes needs more than just good teaching. Everyone needs to have a clear understanding of the school's expectations.

A lack of clarity can lead to conflict, as each party makes different assumptions about what is acceptable and what is not. This inevitably means that you need to develop a series of routines and procedures that cover all aspects of school life. Of course, armed with this long list of policies, there is always the danger that the whole school community becomes overwhelmed by the sheer number of rules and regulations. The very best schools get the balance right.

One way around this is to have a set of generic principles that underpin the way the school operates. The notion of mutual respect is as good a place to start as any. The key question is: where do we draw the line between what is and what isn't acceptable? My own experience has taught me that pupils will always nudge their way up to the line wherever it is placed. What the very best schools do is put the line somewhere that says to pupils, parents and teachers at the school that it expects only the highest of standards. These schools fight any battles in this territory. There is nothing more effective than this setting of the highest of expectations and sticking to them in every aspect of the work of the school.

The evidence has shown that once the overall expectations have been agreed, great schools then break these down into more specific areas. For example, using a series of levels to define positive and negative behaviours, then setting out how a school should respond to them, can create clarity around how situations should be dealt with. Increasingly, I have seen the number of levels within classroom management protocols reducing in schools I work with. In other words, there is a faster escalation of consequences.

Clarity brings freedom to take risks and experiment
One could be forgiven for thinking that clarity around pedagogy and behaviour management systems ought to be a prerequisite of good schools and therefore, given the remit of this publication is maybe not the business of a book looking at what leaders at all levels do to create great schools. However, a common thread running through so many great schools we heard from on the G2G programme, supported by much reading, is that it is the clarity of these systems and expectations that allows schools the security to take risks and experiment, understanding that these journeys into the unknown are underpinned by the solid foundations that clear systems can bring.

The very best schools are highly creative both in developing classroom practice and in the way that they encourage students to experiment and express themselves freely, often exposing themselves emotionally to their peers. Creativity can flourish when the right preconditions are in place that make students feel comfortable and supported. The most successful schools will trial new processes and ideas, safe in the knowledge that business as usual will continue as a result of the hard work that has gone into creating a shared way of working understood by the whole school community.

The importance of keeping focused

The final point to make about clarity of vision and strategy is around the benefits that can come from having a clear view about what a school focuses on and therefore, by definition, what it decides not to do. As Stephen Covey (2004) suggests, "The main thing is to keep the main thing the main thing"!

A clear message from many of the successful schools I have worked with has been that they are very good at distinguishing between those things that help them achieve their core purpose and those that may run the risk of dilution of their intent. We all know the temptation to engage with every initiative, particularly when inspection frameworks and other national expectations may encourage schools to do so.

Those schools that have a well-developed set of goals are well placed to make decisions about these possible areas of development. But the very best schools will not only have clarity around their goals, but will also have developed a clear understanding throughout the institution of how those goals are achieved. It is against these ways of working that judgements can be made about whether a particular initiative would be worthwhile.

As Peter Matthews puts it, "characteristically, these schools are able to maintain a sharp focus, rigour and consistency in the basics, while innovating and developing their provision further to bring new gains in pupils' learning and achievement. They do not overstretch themselves and are careful not to jump on bandwagons. Middle and senior leaders have a thorough understanding of which developments are right for their school and which are not. They scrutinise new ideas and developments and ask hard questions about what value they will have for students' learning and achievement."

Crucially, these leaders also understand how much capacity the school has to support innovation and development (and they actively work to strengthen it). Whilst the schools are not afraid to take risks, the risks that they do take are careful, calculated and considered. Anything that is done is carefully planned and meticulously implemented.'

In other words, the absolute focus on the core business of the school is maintained. Innovation, creativity and risk-taking are encouraged, but only when they help deliver the clearly identified goals for the school.

An evidence-based approach

Much has been written recently about teaching becoming a more evidence-based profession. Without evidence, we have no empirical proof that strategies and interventions work, we only have individual opinion and judgement. For too long, our judgements about which reading strategies work or which class size is most effective have been based on incorrect assumptions developed by teachers and leaders from just their personal experience without consideration of other evidence.

An evidence-based approach is about combining one's own experience, observation and analysis with what other external evidence suggests. That way you can work out what is going to work for your pupils in your context. It is also about making sure you don't adopt any externally generated idea without first checking out its credentials. For example, there are two ideas that have swept education over the past decade: visual, audio and kinaesthetic (VAK) learning styles (Fleming 2001) and Brain Gym (Educational Kinesiology Foundation). Both were thought to tap into the way pupils learn to help them improve cognition and outcomes. Both were taken by thousands of schools as an answer to pupil engagement and learning. But subsequent research has suggested there is little basis for these ideas (Coffield, 2004).

As teachers and leaders, we often base our strategies and interventions on personal experience, or what we have seen work. This is why middle leaders can sometimes feel that more experienced members of staff who have seen more and have more experience, believe they know more or can tell them why something will not work. In reality though, it is hard to know without also looking at the evidence. Good strategies might be considered not to work because the teacher implemented them poorly. Evidence gives you the proof and grounding to have confidence in your strategy, an empirical basis to disprove the doubters and a means to get the whole team to focus on what works.

Accessing evidence is becoming easier. The two most useful sources of evidence are John Hattie's *Visible Learning* (2009) and the Education

Endowment Foundation's (EEF) *Toolkit*. The two are connected and give effect sizes (a measure of how effective an intervention is) for a range of pupil interventions from class size and homework, to assessment for learning. The EEF toolkit also gives relative cost and value for money data so you can judge which interventions to use. The Education Endowment Foundation disseminates the results from the evaluations it has run.

Key points

- Are you clear about exactly what you are trying to achieve and the two or three key elements of your work that will enable you to achieve it?

- Are governors or trustees at the heart of the development of your strategic approach and the monitoring of its implementation and impact?

- Is the concept of OST (objective-strategy-tactics) something that might be useful for you to adopt in your context?

- Do you need to develop a clear pedagogical approach?

- Do you have clear systems and procedures in place to manage behaviour effectively, thus creating a positive climate for learning?

- Are you good at rejecting initiatives that may distract you from your focus?

- Are you clear about your core principles and do you set the highest expectations in all aspects of your work?

- Do you provide opportunities for your staff to work collaboratively on properly evaluated school-based innovation for improvement?

- Do you provide systematic opportunities for staff to share learning based on research and evidence with one another?

- Do you run school-based research and trials based upon a disciplined approach to design, implementation and review?

- Do leaders at all level take decisions based on internal and external research and evidence?

Chapter Eight

Creating alignment

Setting an example is not the main means of
influencing others; it is the only means.
Albert Einstein

As I mentioned in the introduction, you can have a great group of staff
that are really motivated and love their jobs, but if they aren't pulling
together in pursuit of a set of shared goals and with a shared strategy,
you just won't achieve as much. That's why alignment matters so much
for leaders at every level. How you achieve this will, of course, depend on
your context. But however you achieve it, having a clear set of strategies
that underpin the culture you want to create and a group of people who
are bought into that approach is at the heart of great delivery in schools.

There is a range of things you can do to create alignment within your
staff team. This chapter will examine some of those ideas. At the heart
of alignment is great communication, which is of course about clarity of
message but also about listening and observing carefully. It is therefore
really important to remember that communication is a two way process;
it's not just about what you say but, equally importantly, what you hear
and observe.

Promoting clarity

An important role for communication is to set out expectations. This leads to greater clarity and hence greater consistency in the way that schools operate. The best school leaders continually reinforce their expectations. They talk about them at every opportunity. They continually show staff they value and appreciate the contribution that an individual may be making.

On a day-to-day basis, when these leaders are walking around school they are looking for things to praise and comment on, both with students and staff. The odd passing comment can mean a great deal to the individuals concerned and they can go on to have a better day as a result.

It also reinforces to others what matters and what is important. This drip-feeding of expectations as part of everyday interactions can be very powerful.

Sometimes it is the quiet word to one side that is most effective, particularly if one knows the person doesn't like receiving praise publicly. For others, it is the public thanks at weekly briefing that is most important. Again, this not only motivates the individual concerned but also sends a message to other colleagues about what is important and valued.

However, the most powerful way to praise is often through writing to colleagues. A handwritten note to someone, a copy to go on that member of staff's personnel file, shows that a school leader has taken the time and seen it as important to sit down and make a point of doing something personal.

In terms of motivating staff and gaining their loyalty, the use of a personal note is probably one of the most effective ways of using praise to communicate and reinforce expectations.

Engaging others in creating the vision and strategy

If you have the time, it usually well worth designing a process that enables all interested parties to have a stake in helping to shape your vision and strategy. If people have had a say in determining where you want to go and how you might get there together, there is a much greater chance they will deliver their own part of the plan when it comes to making things happen and, more importantly, happen to a high standard. In some ways, this is actually more relevant in schools than it is in some other workplaces, simply because teachers are so often operating solo. Even in schools where people are popping in and out of lessons, teachers are often left to their own devices for much of their working day. In these circumstances, people need to be intrinsically motivated to do a great job as there is usually no-one else there checking up on them who can offer the extrinsic carrot or stick.

Inspiring others

But people need to feel more than just consulted. All leaders need to offer inspiration to the teams they lead. It is a critical part of what you need to do if you are to achieve your goals and have the impact you are seeking for pupils. First and foremost, people will be inspired by your passion and commitment. So modelling what you expect others to do, to a high standard and with energy, is a great way to influence others and gain alignment. Setting a good example is a great way to get buy-in.

But there are a number of subtle ways you can inspire others. Valuing others' contributions, particularly when they demonstrate discretionary effort or particularly effective performance, will inspire. Inspiration is as important in daily communication just as much as at the 'key moments' – like the first team meeting in September. If a group of staff trust you and feel inspired by you, they will usually do as they are asked to, no matter what they feel about what has been suggested. On the other hand, you can have the greatest idea in the world, but if you have failed to inspire or argue persuasively, few will deliver for you.

Leaders new to role, can sometimes find themselves working with a group of staff where results have been poor for the last few years, where there is poor teaching and learning and where both pupils and staff almost seem to drag their feet as they arrive. It can feel like an impossible task to get to where you want to be. In your head, you can see the brilliant learning environments, inspirational teaching and smart enthusiastic engaged learners, but how do you get everyone to see that vision?

Your ability to communicate and articulate exactly what you want is crucial. Your presentation skills are important and you need to consider how you come across. It cannot be a jumbled mass of thoughts as these will conceal the key messages. Clearly defined pictures of success and the exact map of how to get there will reassure and motivate your team. Giving yourself a chance to rehearse this sort of presentation privately with someone you trust is a great way to make sure you make the most of these set-piece opportunities.

Presentations are a powerful way to engage each and every person, but consideration should be given to the fact that this can look different for different people. As before, knowing your context matters. A well-planned presentation ensures that, by the end, each person knows their role in the vision, their part in the team, knows that they are highly valued and knows that they are completing the task for excellent reasons. They know that their team leader has complete confidence in their ability to make a difference. The team is clear about what success looks like and what the timeline expectations are. They feel that they have the capability to complete the task with confidence because their leader believes in them.

Integrity

As Stephen Covey (2006) points out in *Speed of Trust*, it is really important that leaders are honest and tell the truth. They don't try to create false impressions or spin the truth. Not only does this build trust but it supports the creation of transparency and develops a culture where it is okay to talk about things that may not be working as well as they might. It is important in these situations to use simple language to describe things as they are and not to manipulate people or distort the facts.

There can sometimes be the temptation to work to hidden agendas or to keep certain facts or viewpoints from people, sometimes even with their best interests at heart. In this context straight talking can often take courage and this will be explored in a later chapter.

But there is clear evidence to suggest that schools that make the most progress don't allow issues to be swept under the carpet. They see problems that are openly talked about and shared with individuals and groups as opportunities for improvement. This creates honest dialogue and greater alignment.

How things are said

How such issues are raised, however, is also very important. Care needs to be taken to pitch what is being said appropriately. Put too gently, the point of what is being said may be lost. Put too bluntly, and any opportunity to change behaviour or move a situation forward may be missed.

Developing the skill to get this balance right is not easy and is another example of where leaders need to not only be very self-aware but also attuned to the needs and situation of those they are communicating with. Making the space to step back and reflect in these circumstances is also important. Too often the temptation is to rush into a conversation without really thinking through what will be most effective.

Influencing others

You are, like anyone in a leadership role, completely reliant upon other people to get the job done. For this reason, your ability to influence others is crucial. Not only do you need to be able to generate enthusiasm and excitement in the things that you want your team to achieve together, you also need to be able to influence others outside the team who may have an indirect influence or impact on your work.

This matters in a number of ways. Depending on your role, you may, for example, want to implement a new curriculum for a year group, introduce a new behaviour system for the whole school or establish a new phonics scheme. Each of these will require buy-in from your staff. Of course you can insist upon individuals implementing whatever they decide they want to set up, but unless your staff are convinced of the benefits of any change or new approach, one can be sure discretionary effort will be lower and the subsequent impact significantly reduced. Being able to effectively influence members of your team will play a key role in ensuring changes are effectively introduced.

For middle leaders in particular, being able to influence externally is also very important. Take, for example, decisions that others may take that have a direct effect on your team. You may wish to have an influence around decisions being made regarding whole school systems for rewarding pupil achievement and behaviour. Or you may be keen to influence how teaching assistants are deployed within your key stage or department. Or you may want a say around the construction of the whole-school timetable. In all these cases, decisions are being taken by others, often in your senior leadership team, that will have a direct effect on the work of your team. For this reason alone, it is important that you are able to exert influence when these decisions are taken. Yes, of course your line manager can act as your advocate if needed. But the more you are able to handle these discussions yourself, the better.

Most school leaders are already very good at influencing others. It is, of course, a skill that all leaders develop very early in their careers, as it's precisely what you do day-in day-out with the pupils you teach! But taking some time to think more systematically about how you influence others can pay dividends.

Degrees of influence

First of all, you can think though the different degrees of influence you may be able to exert. Those whom you directly line manage are to some extent under your control although, as already discussed, getting buy-in from others, even where a command and control approach is possible, is still by far the most effective approach. Then there are those on whom you can have a direct influence on but don't directly line manage. If you have a role in coordinating literacy across an area or some form of pastoral or achievement role, for example, you may well have a team of individuals where you are not the formal line manager. Then there are those where your influence may be indirect, where your ability to influence is dependent upon someone else. And then there are those over whom you just need to accept you have no opportunity to influence whatsoever. Knowing this can save an awful lot of time and wasted energy. The more senior your role, whilst you have more hierarchical control in theory, the more it will usually only be indirectly through others that you can exert that influence.

How you approach influencing someone therefore needs to reflect the degree of influence you have. You can clearly afford to be far more assertive and directive with those under your control or over whom you have some direct influence. For those over whom you only have an indirect influence, you will usually need to adopt a subtler and less assertive approach.

Choosing how to influence

But there is another consideration. You need to think about the range of different ways in which you can influence others. Choosing the right approach will depend, once again, upon both the context and the person you are trying to influence. Some situations are best handled with a straightforward and carefully thought through logical argument. In situations where the facts really do speak for themselves and the person you are seeking to influence is attracted by a logical argument, this is clearly going to be the right approach to adopt.

However, that knowledge about the person whom you are seeking to influence is critical because, for some people, the logic of an argument could be beaten, for example, by a more values-based pitch into the discussion you're engaging in. Trying to use a logical argument with someone who is approaching an issue from a more emotional perspective is clearly not the best way of successfully influencing their view or decision.

You may also want to consider how much you're prepared to negotiate around a particular issue. This is particularly useful in situations where you have something that may be of value to those whom you seek to influence, for example. You may have at your disposal financial resource. Or you may be able to influence someone else on his or her behalf. This 'you scratch my back, I'll scratch yours' approach can be a very powerful way of influencing some people. Of course, others may find it rather distasteful and be much more persuaded by an argument that appeals to their sense of moral purpose.

Others can simply be persuaded by passion, energy and enthusiasm for a new idea. These are people who relish change, like to be in the thick of the action, and don't want to spend too long thinking through all the options.

A skilful influencer, therefore, will be thinking about the extent of their influence, the context of the issue under discussion, and the likely response from individuals you're trying to persuade. You probably already instinctively take these factors into consideration when persuading others. But taking time to properly think through how you might approach a particular issue is usually time well spent.

Taking time to identify those individuals who might be key to influencing others on your behalf is also very useful. Just like with groups of pupils, there will usually be a few of your colleagues whom others tend to look up to or admire. Or it may just be they can be very vocal in the staffroom! Either way, in certain circumstances there is much to be gained by getting these opinion formers around to your way of thinking and allowing them to then do your work for you in influencing others. Of course, this is often far from easy and may well not be appropriate or desirable in many situations.

So there is lots you can do. But it's also really important for you to know when to stop. Continuing to try and influence people when it is clear that they're not engaging can often be counter-productive and cause others to dig their heels in. It can also mean that, on a future occasion, your ability to influence is diminished. It's a bit of a cliché, but losing the battle for the long-term goal of winning the war can be a short-term price that's worth paying.

Managing up

When people talk about managing up, they often have some sense that this is about an individual trying to manipulate their boss in some way or even to convince them to do something that they otherwise wouldn't do! Managing up is therefore seen as somehow slightly dishonest or underhand. But actually, nothing could be further from the truth. Managing up is all about making sure that you have a productive relationship with your line manager that supports both of you to achieve the shared goals for the pupils you both serve. It's about you taking your share of responsibility for the quality of your joint working relationship so you can both work towards mutually agreed goals that are in the best interests of you, your line manager and your school. It isn't political manoeuvring.

The benefits of managing up

If you are good at managing up, you and your manager both stand to benefit in a whole range of different ways. Not only are you more likely to get the kind of resources that you need, you will also have created a strong working relationship that benefits you both. So, getting that relationship right is in everyone's interests. Like a great marriage, though, it takes work from both parties!

For middle leaders in particular, having a good relationship with your line manager also gives you a direct route into the senior team of the school. Not only can this lead to improved opportunities for you to gain experience beyond your current role, it is also a really good way to help make sure that the members of your own team are on the radar of your senior colleagues. In other words, managing up is all about creating positive, mutually beneficial relationships for you, your team and the organisation as a whole.

So what does managing up actually involve?

There are a number of practical things you can do to strengthen your relationship with your line manager. First of all, how well aware are you of their expectations of you? Similarly, have you clearly articulated the expectations that you have of them? For example, do you know how your line manager likes to receive information and how often? Do they prefer a regular e-mail update, or are they actually happy to let you get on with things on the basis that you will only get in touch if there's something you think they need to know?

In terms of your own needs, have you talked to them about the ways that you like to work and the things that you find energising? Do they know those that can have a negative impact on your effectiveness at work? This is where using simple psychometric tools, such as those we offer at Leadership Matters, can be enormously useful. Beginning to articulate the things that motivate each of you can quickly lead to more productive working relationships. As a line manager yourself, you may want to think about how you can enable these important conversations to happen with those you manage.

Secondly, when you are faced with an issue or concern, making sure you don't just arrive at their door with a problem, but come with possible solutions and ideas about how the problem can be solved is usually welcomed.

Thirdly, if there are issues that are concerning you or if there are disagreements between you and your manager, it is usually beneficial for you both to try and address these sooner rather than later. It may well be the case that your line manager is blissfully unaware that you have a particular concern or worry. Getting these things out in the open as soon as they arise is both beneficial to your relationship in the long-run, but also enables these issues to be dealt with before they become an even bigger problem.

Fourthly, it's really important for you to be as honest with your line manager as you can about everything. Their trust in you can very quickly be eroded if they discover you've tried to hide something from them or have distorted the truth. It's also important to remember that trust is more than just a measure of personal integrity, it's also about someone's view of a person's competence. This means you should think about how you can give your line manager reassurance that you know what you're doing and that you're delivering results. Taking opportunities in meetings with them to present well-organised data and other information combined with good planning and personal organisation will give them confidence that you're on top of the job.

To sum up, when it comes to creating alignment, as the quotation from Albert Einstein at the beginning of this chapter reminds us, never underestimate the power of leading by example. If you can demonstrate through your own actions the success of an idea, properly implemented, others will follow. It comes as a surprise to most leaders, whatever role they are undertaking, just how much others notice the things that they do and say. It is no good saying to others that it is important to always challenge students if they are shouting in the corridor and then failing to do so as a leader. The old adage that 'it is not what you say but what you do that counts' sums up beautifully how this form of communication is crucial. One's behaviour can either powerfully reinforce expectations or quickly destroy them. This will either build or erode the trust and motivation of colleagues.

For precisely this reason, it is critical that you make sure you really do offer strong exemplification of what you wish others to do. To say one thing and do another is usually extremely dispiriting and is very likely to lead to poor implementation by others.

Summary

- Do you take time to keep your messages simple and listen and observe carefully?
- Do you need to engage with staff in shaping the vision and strategy so that you get greater buy-in?
- Think about the strategies and opportunities you have to inspire others. Do you always make the most of them?
- What strategies do you use to influence others?
- Are these adjusted to the context or the person?
- Do you keep your messages simple?
- Do you model what excellence looks like?
- Do you make the time to consciously manage your relationship with your line manager?
- Do you model and exemplify what you expect others to do?

Chapter Nine

Building and sustaining relationships

I suppose leadership at one time meant muscles;
but today it means getting along with people.
Mahatma Gandhi

Building and sustaining relationships is one of the most important elements of any leader's role. As the popular quote attributed to Peter Drucker says: "Culture eats strategy for breakfast". Although he is using culture here as something more akin to culture and climate combined in my definition, the point is that you can have the greatest strategy in the world, but if relationships between you and your staff and amongst themselves aren't good, then delivery and pupil outcomes won't be what you want them to be.

Demonstrating respect

Stephen Covey (2006) is very clear in his *Speed of trust* about how the best leaders genuinely care for others and are naturally happy to show that they care in an open way. They respect the dignity of all the staff no matter what their role in school. Taking time to have a conversation with the caretaker who has a bad back during exam season is just as important as comforting a deputy head who may have suffered a personal loss.

School leaders who take the time and trouble to do something to support a colleague, or who take a personal interest in a particular pupil who is dealing with some really tough problems at home, sends a clear message to the whole school community that people matter to you. You can so easily become embroiled with your own problems on a day-to-day basis that it is all too easy to forget about how important it is to get these things right.

Sending a card wishing someone well, or organising some flowers to be sent takes a few minutes to put in place, but can mean so much to the individual concerned. But taking this trouble does more than just support that individual. The message that colleagues matter as people and not just as employees doesn't just go out to the individual concerned; it permeates the whole institution. That buys loyalty and commitment. It reinforces the ethos that staff and pupils are valued. It makes the school a place that people are proud to belong to, proud to be a part of.

The cumulative effect of lots of small acts of kindness is immeasurable. The little things that leaders do can build morale and a sense of trust. They play a significant role in developing momentum. If people feel valued and cared for they reflect that by valuing and caring for the place they work in and the people they work for.

If you also model that behaviour to pupils in school, they in turn gain greater trust in you and a sense of belonging to their school. It is a very simple, virtuous cycle that leaders need to remind themselves of frequently, particularly during times of stress when it becomes far more likely that the importance of respect and dignity become overlooked.

Many of the best schools I have worked with also make important statements about how they value their staff more generally. For example, some of these schools provide free tea and coffee in the staffroom at break-time, even though pressures on budgets are always tight. Others offer a free lunch for those staff sitting with students at lunchtime or who are running a club. These gestures are highly symbolic and represent a powerful way of building momentum and helping create a climate where people naturally begin to act in a self-disciplined way because they feel valued.

In one school, the senior team goes to great lengths to ensure staff are, in their words, cherished. This doesn't look the same for everyone. The school believes it is vital that the senior team carefully works out a personalised plan for each member of staff that ensures that they feel valued and nurtured. Part of this involves ensuring every exceptional deed is personally recognised by the head.

The same school also ensures that relaxation is valued. Monday breakfasts, Friday cakes, fruit bowls and chocolates delivered to offices, end of term celebrations, social events, prizes and celebrations for attendance, great practice and team spirit are all part of the mix. The head even says to the staff 'if you hear of anything another school does that means that they care more, then tell us and we will do it!'

Showing loyalty

We have already talked about the fact that all schools and individuals can face challenges and difficult times. What good leaders appear to do in these circumstances is keep faith with the individuals that make it successful. There is a clear link here with developing a 'no-blame' culture. Just because someone has made a mistake with the timetable or said something inappropriate to a student or parent, doesn't mean leaders should suddenly forget the important contribution that the particular individual makes. In fact, quite the reverse is usually true. In these situations, what staff need to know is that they are supported and trusted and that they can be trusted to learn from their mistake and move forward.

In contrast, when things are going well, the very best leaders generously give credit to all those who have enabled that success to happen. There is nothing more disheartening and likely to reduce trust than for an individual to see a leader take credit for something someone else did. Openly acknowledging the contribution of others is critical.

Loyal leaders will also speak up for an individual even when they may not be present and even if it may be uncomfortable to do so. Rest assured, word will get back and the person concerned will feel even more valued and motivated than they did before. This, in turn, builds momentum and alignment towards the school's goals.

Loyal leaders also resist the temptation to 'bad-mouth' colleagues behind their backs. As mentioned previously, they respect the individual concerned by dealing directly, raising any concerns they may have face-to-face. They don't say: 'I'm not saying anything I wouldn't say to them myself.' They keep such matters private, however tempting it may be to talk about such issues.

Keeping commitments

One of the most frustrating things for members of staff in any school is when someone senior doesn't keep a promise made. It is probably the quickest way that trust can be destroyed. Yet honouring commitments, especially when it is clearly difficult to do so, is also one of the most effective ways you can build confidence and trust with staff, pupils and parents.

Leaders can often be tempted to 'wriggle out' of commitments that they may have made. Often this will arise in situations where a promise is given before thinking through all its implications.

For example, a head who agrees, as a result of some special pleading, that a particular member of staff may have a reduced timetabled commitment may well find themselves in the position where other staff complain this is unfair. The temptation, of course, is to renege on the promise made. Yet it is probably wiser to honour the original agreement and openly apologise to the other colleagues that an error had been made which will be rectified in future. The ability to say sorry and acknowledge the error is critical here. Trying to make excuses and blame changing circumstances can be tempting but reduces trust.

This example also serves to illustrate the importance of carefully thinking through commitments and promises before making them.

Keeping reflective and creating time to think

In a later chapter, we explore the issue of developing people. Part of this analysis includes an acknowledgement of the importance of creating a culture where your staff are constantly learning on the job. School leaders are no different and should take the opportunity to model this behaviour and lead by example.

Having a reflective approach to the job and a willingness to listen to other colleagues is critical. Remembering the importance of asking the right questions rather than being expected to know the answers fits with this approach.

Many school leaders I coach find this is a very useful way to support this process of reflection. Having quality time set aside, supported by someone with the right skills, can often make a real difference in helping leaders think through complex challenges.

An appreciation of the importance of learning about the personalities of those we manage is also helpful. Whilst it is important not to overplay this, it is again useful to employ some flexibility around how you manage different individuals. For example, most schools have members of staff who are natural followers of systems and procedures but sometimes find it hard to see the bigger picture. They can easily become obsessed with the most unimportant of scenarios, even becoming quite stressed.

Compare this with those individuals who are great at thinking out-of-the-box, but have a much more laissez-faire approach to certain situations which can undermine and frustrate colleagues when they don't follow school procedures properly. Both types of colleague require a response, but the nature of that response should reflect what school leaders have learnt about the individuals concerned, in particular their personality.

In general terms, however, the important thing is that school leaders don't stop reflecting or learning. You look after your own personal and professional development. You make time to step back and see the bigger picture.

Your relationship with governors

So often leaders in schools reduce their capacity to think in a strategic way because they don't give themselves time to think, reflect and grow as a leader. The best leaders I work with have understood this and don't feel guilty about making quality time to reflect. If you are a head or system leader, investing time in building your relationship with your governors or trustees can be a really effective way to step back and take the strategic view. Your relationship with your chair has the potential to be particularly useful in this regard. Having the opportunity to build an open, honest and trusting relationship with your chair will allow for healthy debate, challenge and recognition, all of which will make you more effective. Apart from anything else, it helps reduce that sense that it's 'lonely at the top'.

Collaboration with leaders across more than one school

When it comes to making time and space to think strategically, one great way to do this is through working with other schools. If you have the opportunity to meet colleagues from other institutions, not only do you learn a lot from them, you inevitably reflect on your own context from a slightly different viewpoint.

Great schools are not islands. They see themselves as having a bigger role than within their own institution. This not only includes the support they provide for their immediate local community; it includes wider support for other schools in the system. These schools also acknowledge the benefits that this outreach work brings back to their own institution. Linked to this, as a school leader, you are very clear about the fact that you don't have the answers to all questions and are constantly seeking to improve and innovate by learning from others outside your own immediate context.

Setting up relationships with leaders in other schools isn't easy and takes time. There are sometimes local tensions that arise from competition for pupils, or even staff, that make it even more difficult. But where mutual benefit can be derived, there is a growing body of evidence that it is worth school leaders spending time to build relationships with other schools both informally and as part of more formal collaborations such as teaching school alliances, trusts or other networks. In any inter-school collaboration, it is important to not just drift into these relationships. There are some key questions to consider:

1. What is the shared purpose for the partnership? What is the driver?

2. What is the partnership aiming to actually do?

3. What does the leadership of the partnership look like and where does it come from?

4. What are the boundaries of the partnership and what is the governance?

5. How does the partnership fit within the wider context and other partnerships?

When it comes to reviewing how well your partnership is working, whether that be as part of a formal group of schools or as a looser alliance or network, you might also find the work of David Hargreaves (2011) really useful. He has created what is effectively an audit tool for school partnerships. You can access this resource via the Leadership Matters website or through the reference section at the end of this book. Figure 12 is my attempt at summarising his thinking.

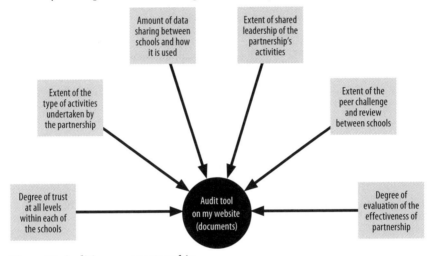

Figure 12: Auditing your partnership
Based on a think-piece by David Hargreaves (2011)

Managing conflict

Both within wider partnerships and within your own team, if a key part of your role is to build and sustain relationships, there are inevitably times when you have to step in to manage conflict. Whilst conflict is usually something that has negative consequences, it can also be a productive way to move a situation forward if handled carefully.

Conflict can arise in a whole range of different ways and with people from outside your own team as well as those from within. Conflict can often arise because of resourcing issues. For example, someone may have a disagreement with a colleague about how much funding a particular course needs to run successfully; or they may be unhappy about the progress the pupils taught by a particular teacher are making. Conflict can also arise because of disagreements about who should be doing what. A lack of clarity on roles within your team can lead to people vying for position, particularly if there are people who are positioning themselves for promotion or other recognition. A classic example is when they end up having two people who are both organising the same thing, such as an assembly or a meeting agenda or an important whole-school initiative, where neither wants to cede ownership of the project.

How should you respond to conflict?

First of all, it is really important to appreciate that context is the critical factor here. Taking time to reflect on the type of conflict is an important first step. Is the disagreement a result of resource, a power-struggle, a difference in values or a personality clash? Or is there something else at play? Working this out first can usually be very helpful in deciding on how to manage the situation.

In doing this, it is helpful to avoiding making too many assumptions about people's motivations. In working out the best way to handle a situation, it is usually well worth having conversations with the individuals concerned to try to understand their positions more accurately.

It is also really important for you to know yourself well. We all have ways in which we tend to respond in conflict situations, usually without really being aware of this. Taking time to reflect on this can also be helpful, as we all have to guard against the tendency to just dive in to try to solve a problem using the same old strategy, regardless of the context.

Choosing the right strategy

Kilmann's (1974) model of conflict management sets out five ways you can respond to or manage conflict below/overleaf.

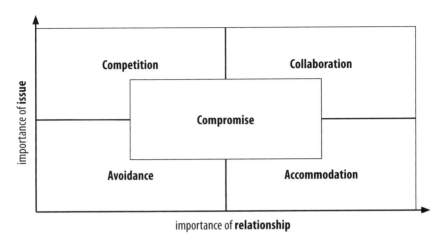

Figure 13: Five approaches to managing conflict
Thomas Kilmann

In each case, there is a different blend of the extent to which the response meets the needs (and tackles the issue), as opposed to the needs of the person or people one is in conflict with (and giving greater importance to maintaining relationships). Figure 13 shows the interrelationship between these elements.

For example, if your sense of the situation is such that someone in a team is attempting to test your authority in some way, for whatever reason, you may decide the appropriate response is to entirely focus on meeting your own needs and pay no regard to their perspective. Such an approach is often known as 'forcing' or 'competing'. In this situation you will firmly pursue your concern despite any resistance from the other person. This type of approach has the advantage of usually providing a quick resolution to conflict or disagreement and can establish your authority not only with the individual concerned but also with the team or staff as a whole. However, taking this approach can sometimes cause the other person to react even more negatively and you need to be prepared to deal with that. It goes without saying, however, that these sorts of conversations are usually best done privately.

In contrast, there can be occasions when it is actually much better to completely back down from a position and concede on the issue being discussed. This can often be a useful tactic when the issue means more to others than it does to you, whilst giving you the opportunity to demonstrate that you can be reasonable, listen to arguments presented and don't just assume that you are always right. This approach is sometimes known as 'accommodating' or 'smoothing'. If used too often, however, you run the risk that your supporters may start to lose faith in your authority or ability to take decisions. Once again, you need to use your own professional judgement about when it is right to back down on an issue.

There are some areas of conflict, however, like choosing a syllabus or curriculum or designing an assessment system, where you would ideally like to find a way forward that all parties are happy with and that doesn't compromise your core beliefs. This 'win-win' approach, or 'collaborating', is a chance to come to a mutually beneficial result in which the underlying concerns of all parties have been met. This approach usually takes time and requires a high level of trust between all involved so that you can work through any feelings of animosity. It has the benefit, if carried out successfully, that you gain the reputation of being a successful negotiator; you build mutual trust and respect in your staff and the shared sense of ownership. However, this approach can be very time-consuming and may not be practical when a quick solution or fast response is required. And it doesn't always work. Again, you need to make a judgment about whether going for a collaborative approach is worth the effort.

Another way to respond to a conflict is to simply ignore it! This is known as 'avoiding' or 'withdrawing'. This can be appropriate if the issue is trivial and simply not worth the effort or when there are other more pressing issues that need to be dealt with. Sometimes you may wish to simply postpone a response because it is not the right time or place to confront a particular issue. This approach can also buy you some time before deciding how to respond. On the other hand, you need to be aware that supporters in your team can see avoiding a particular conflict as a sign of weakness. Using withdrawing strategies without negatively affecting your own position does require skill and experience.

The fifth approach to managing conflict sits right in the middle of each of the four already mentioned and is unsurprisingly called 'compromising'. Compromising looks for a mutually acceptable solution that partially satisfies all or both parties in a particular conflict. Again you will need to make the call in the context of your particular situation about whether accepting a compromise is the right way forward. It can often be a first step to building trust with staff and has the advantage of usually quickly resolving the situation.

Some of these strategies are easier and more tempting than others, particularly if you are new in post. Avoiding an issue or smoothing over can be the path of least resistance. But as the old saying goes, 'there's no pain without gain'. Sometimes you just need to have the courage to do the right thing.

Not forgetting to have some fun!

Schools can often be stressful places. External expectations seem to grow every year. Staff and pupils work increasingly long hours in pursuit of their goals. In such circumstances, it can be easy to forget the importance of having fun. Seeing the funny side of difficult situations, playing the odd harmless practical joke or just remembering not to take everything too seriously is essential.

For school leaders this principle can operate on two levels. Firstly, it can permeate all the everyday interactions. Clearly there are some leaders for whom this will be easier than for others. Cracking a joke or making a witty comment is the bread and butter of some of the best leaders at all levels.

However, this can't be about individuals trying to be something that they're not. Keeping a frame of mind where one tries to raise a smile can be important in lifting spirits and making work a more fun place to be, but it needs to be genuine and heartfelt. You need to be true to yourself but give yourself permission to have a bit of fun now and again.

Secondly, schools need to plan for plenty of occasions where staff can socialise together and enjoy themselves in a more relaxed environment. It is a chance for you to show your staff team that they are valued and respected, but it is also another way to build relationships and make sure people have fun together. Of course, this can be organised by middle leaders in sub-teams as well as by more senior staff for whole-school events.

The dividend from spending resource on providing for some special occasions will usually reap huge rewards. It builds trust, momentum and a sense of well-being, all of which build a school's capacity to develop its people.

The importance of the little things

My own experience of working with thousands of school leaders over the years has taught me that none of us realises the impact of our own day-to-day personal behaviours and organisational skills. For example, there is nothing more frustrating for colleagues than leaders who:

1. don't reply to a letter or e-mail within a day or two of it being sent;

2. regularly turn up late to teach or to meetings because they have been dealing with 'more important' matters;

3. leave colleagues out of the loop regarding a particular issue or event;

4. forget to do things that they said they would do or even do something differently from that which had been previously agreed;

5. ask for feedback at the end of event and then fail to act upon it or even acknowledge the feedback the next time the event is organised;

6. don't meet deadlines that all staff are expected to meet;

7. make (often poor) decisions 'on the hoof' because they have failed to plan ahead effectively.

Not only do badly organised leaders have a direct negative impact on the areas they are managing, they also have an impact on leadership capacity more widely. Their ability to inspire and motivate is diminished; they don't have the same level of credibility with colleagues and morale is inevitably lower. Staff start to feel disenchanted and question why they should go the extra mile when their line manager doesn't appear to value them. Of course, most of the time, nothing could be further from the truth. School leaders do value their colleagues; it's just that the implicit messages sent out by poor organisational skills might suggest that the focus on personal performance needs to be increased.

But where things do go wrong, the best leaders are up front in saying so. They take responsibility for not delivering and talk about what they need to do differently in the future. This openness helps to build trust and transparency.

Key points

- Do you show respect for everyone you work with, regardless of their role?
- Are you loyal to colleagues, even when it is difficult to be so?
- Do you always keep your promises?
- Is your personal organisation good enough? It matters to others more than you probably realise.
- Do you have good partnerships with other leaders beyond your own school?
- Do you manage conflict with others effectively?
- Do you make time to have some fun?!

Chapter Ten

Creating and enabling teams

I'm going to tell you the story about the geese that fly 5,000 miles from Canada to France. They fly in V-formation but the second ones don't fly. They're the subs for the first ones. And then the second ones take over – so it's teamwork.

Alex Ferguson

As a school leader, at whatever level, you will probably be working with a diverse range of individuals. Some of your staff may well be very experienced, extremely confident and need very little support and guidance from you. These individuals have a huge amount to give to the team as a whole. Bringing out the best in your high performers is really important, particularly as the temptation is to focus on those staff who are much less experienced, much less confident and look to you for support and guidance.

Some of your staff may be very aware of their own strengths and weaknesses, whereas others may lack the self-awareness that enables them to see themselves as others do. Some team members may be facing significant external pressures from family or other aspects of their lives.

Some may be highly ambitious individuals; others may be very content with their current role and have no plans to take the next career step.

So that's straightforward then! Your role is to help support these disparate groups of individuals into high performing teams committed to a shared vision, in a way that brings out the best in each of them. What follows is a summary of some of things that can help.

First of all, creating a climate of openness and trust has to be the starting point. If you are to understand what makes others in your team tick, the team needs to feel comfortable and able to share things about one another. If there is one thing, however, that you might want to focus on, it would be making time to have individual one-to-one conversations with members of your team. For some middle leaders, particularly those of you in pastoral roles or where you have responsibility for coordination of a particular area such as literacy and numeracy, finding the time to have even a short one-to-one conversation can sometimes be more challenging than for someone working in a subject department. If you are a senior leader, this can be easier to do. Either way, do really try to make the time, formally or informally, to get to know the members of your team and better understand their strengths and weaknesses.

Of course, more formal appraisal and performance management processes are an important element of this process but the power of the regular, developmental conversation is, in my view, at the heart of what really drives improvement and performance. Taking the time to agree how these conversations will work in practice is in itself an important part of the process. The diagram below describes some of the features of great 1:1 meetings.

1. Agree or **contract** with one another at the start how your 1:1s will work.
2. **Schedule** your 1:1s well in advance and avoid cancelling
3. As you delegate more, let your team members each **create their own agenda** (maybe provide an agenda template to help) – add in your items afterwards. Decide if you will settle the agenda **before or in** the meeting.
4. Avoid the temptation for them to be updates – this can often be done in other ways. Try to make your 1:1s about things that need **discussion**.
5. Ask **questions** more than you give advice. Make your 1:1s **developmental**.

6. Occasionally, **ask for help** with something you are working on that you would value their opinion or help with.
7. Make your 1:1s feel **personal**. Ask them how you can do this.
8. Try to ensure they **leave feeling** valued, energised and positive.
9. If you have any follow-up actions, try to do them the **same day** if you can.
10. Occasionally, **ask for feedback** on your own performance.

Figure 14: Top tips for great 1:1 meetings

You may also find it useful for your team to use a personality tool, such as the one we have developed at Leadership Matters to help you understand one another's personalities as a team, as covered earlier in this book. This doesn't just help you better understand the individuals in your team, it also gives your team members a better understanding of you. Some people find the use of these sorts of tools quite threatening, so taking time to talk through how best to introduce such an idea can be helpful.

Making the most of meetings

A big chunk of this chapter is given over to reflecting on characteristics of effective meetings. The time you spend together with colleagues is precious and usually quite limited. But it has the potential to both support the effective working of a team or, if badly handled, to actually have the reverse effect! In thinking about meetings, it's just as important to remind yourself that what happens before or after a meeting can sometimes be just as important as the things that actually happen in the meeting.

Before a meeting

First of all, make sure you have a clear process for setting an agenda, prioritising items and clarifying who will lead each item. You need to remember, it isn't your job to lead each item. The more others take the lead, the more you will be working as a team rather than as a group of individuals that are doing what they are told. You should aim to make sure each agenda item has a clear time allocation. You should be clear in advance what the outcome required for each item is – for information, discussion, or decision? Ensure you allow sufficient time for people to read papers in advance of the meeting, so that all participants in a meeting can reasonably be expected to have read material before a meeting. Try to predict which areas for discussion may need careful handling and think about whether any pre-discussions may be appropriate.

During a meeting

At the start of the meeting it can sometimes be helpful for a chair to review the agenda and reprioritise if there appears to be insufficient time to cover all the items. When doing this, they should make sure they think about those items that are important, not just those that appear urgent.

You should make sure you have agreed who is going to record any actions from the meeting and who is keeping an eye on timings. Sometimes it makes sense for this to be someone other than the person chairing the meeting. Whoever is chairing the meeting should try to create a climate where everyone has the opportunity to contribute. Sometimes this may mean inviting individuals to make a contribution, particularly if they are less confident or more shy, in a way that won't cause undue embarrassment or resentment.

But the golden rule is to make sure all your meetings finish on time. This will require the whole team to resist the temptation to go off on a tangent or go into too much operational detail. Often, these discussions can be more effectively considered by a smaller group of individuals outside the meeting. When you feel the time is right, you may want to suggest rotating the chair of meetings. This is a powerful way of showing the whole team that they will have an important role to play as well as giving them the opportunity to develop new skills.

At the end of the meeting, if it is helpful, try to take time to review the key actions. Where appropriate, you should agree to the date and time of the next meeting and make sure you finish by thanking all participants and finish on a positive note, however difficult earlier discussions may have been.

1. Be clear what type of meeting it is – *what is it for?*
2. Make sure the *environment* is right; offer refreshments?
3. Don't have a meeting for the *sake of it.*
4. Make sure the *right people* are there; use sub-groups
5. Ensure there is plenty of *notice* of meetings and pre-work
6. Have a *clear agenda* (prioritised; realistic; timed; owned)

7. Agree *meeting protocols* for discussion and stick to them
8. Usually best *not to 'present'* anything – send out pre-reading (in good time) and assume it has been read properly
9. Keep a clear *record* of agreed actions
10. *Chair* should: encourage participation; keep focus; keep to time
11. Mobile technology *protocols* are clear and followed
12. *Rotate* roles of chair and note-taker, where appropriate
13. Clarify *outcomes* at the end and thank everyone
14. Share note of meeting *promptly*, with actions, owners and timelines Use *pre- and post-meeting* discussions to 'oil the wheels'
15. *Participants* should listen, respect others' views, be honest, challenge constructively, respect confidentiality and adhere to cabinet responsibility

Figure 15: Top tips for effective meetings

After a meeting

Stress the importance that the note of actions is agreed and circulated promptly. Where there have been particularly sensitive discussions, consider whether a short post-discussion conversation may be appropriate with any individuals. From time to time, ask people in their team for feedback. What can you do to improve your meetings?

Meeting protocols

Taking some of these ideas a stage further, one strategy I have seen used successfully in a number of schools is developing a protocol for how meetings are conducted that is quite prescriptive about what is almost a meeting pedagogy. Figure 16 gives an example of how one of these works in practice.

Before the meeting
1. Have a mechanism to agree two or three *priority items*
2. Circulate short document that summarises:
    (i) who is the *owner* of the issue;
    (ii) why it is *important*;
    (iii) what the owner wants *help with* (eg. advice for reflection or decision to be made in the meeting)
    (iv) relevant *pre-reading* as background

At the meeting
1. *Brief intro* by owner of the issue
2. Each person, in order, *gives help* asked for
3. Go *round* again
4. *Final* chance for a 'chip in'
5. Owner *summarises* what they are taking away / makes decision

Figure 16: Using a meeting protocol

Getting your meeting structure right

For all leaders, particularly those of you in senior or system leadership roles, one of the challenges can be creating time for strategic discussion. Lenconi (2012) in his book, *The Advantage*, advocates thinking about meetings as being of three distinct types. Figure 17 shows how his approach has been modified by one school I know to suit their particular context.

Daily (No more than 15 minutes)
- Go round each in turn.
- 60 secs *operational* update plus request discussion item
- Agree agenda for short discussion in meeting
- Keep to time (by only briefly discussing priority stuff)

Weekly / fortnightly (No more than 2 hours)
- Clear on purpose/outcome needed in relation to specific *plans*
- Timed and owned
- Papers in advance
- Clarity on how meeting is conducted to ensure max. efficiency
- Agenda next time agreed

Termly (3-6 hours; ideally off-site)
- Same broad approach as for weekly meeting
- But only about creating and/or reviewing *objectives/strategy*

Figure 17: Three types of meeting

Adapted from a model by Lencioni in *The Advantage*

Developing a collaborative approach

Helping the members of a team work together effectively can often involve spotting opportunities for small sub-groups of your team to work together on particular projects. For example, groups of two or three working on curriculum planning or a specific whole-school initiative can be a really powerful way of building relationships within a team as well as playing to the individual strengths of the team as a whole.

The key to making this work, however, is for you to think through carefully who is likely to work well with whom and in which particular area of work. There's nothing worse than asking two people to work together, particularly at an early stage of developing a collaborative approach, if you're not sure they are currently able to work together well. Similarly, if you're delegating a task to a sub-group of the team when they're not confident they have the skills and experience to carry out what is required. This can have the effect of reducing, not increasing, the collaborative spirit within your team.

How well are teams working together?

Whilst ensuring that you are able to make the most of your formal meeting time, taking time out from the day-to-day pressures of your role to reflect upon how your team is working together as a unit can be very productive.

Much has been written about how such high performing teams develop. We all know this doesn't happen overnight and that most teams go through a series of stages before they are really effective. The most well-known model for describing team development was created by Bruce Tuckman (1965), and is summarised by his four stages of *forming, storming, norming* and *performing*. There is a simple logic to his analysis that definitely resonates in a school context. We can all probably think of a team that never got beyond the internal politics and vying for position that characterises the storming phase of a team's development. It is interesting to note that Tuckman suggests trust doesn't appear until the final stage of his model. He would argue that trust takes time to build and is the product of how the team has built relationships over time.

But a more recent model developed by Patrick Lencioni (2002), suggests that for a team to develop, trust actually needs to be there at the very beginning. Without trust, he would argue, team members can't properly debate and argue without it becoming personal, which results in superficial discussion and challenge that leads to poor decision-making and performance. As with Tuckman, this is also a pretty compelling analysis.

A team model for schools

So who is right? Well, in a sense, they both are. If we combine the two, we have a model that starts at the beginning with the formation of a team and goes on to show how a team can, using the trust that has built up, go on to enjoy powerful debate and a shared sense of buy-in into the team's goals as well as the programmes needed to achieve them. In other words, trust is somewhere along the journey, not at the start or the end.

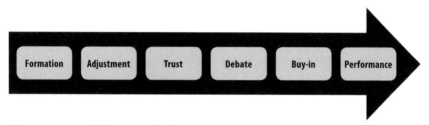

Figure 18: A model for team development

Formation

Early days; getting to know each other; lots of saying the right thing; not rocking the boat; OK but superficial relationships.

Adjustment

Personal views are asserted; people vying for position; lots of assumptions about motives; misunderstanding and bad feeling is not uncommon; difficult time for the leader to manage.

Trust

Trust between team members is developing; they are comfortable in exposing their own worries, fears, vulnerabilities and weaknesses; they are honest with one another; people feel valued, supported and respected by others in the team.

Debate

Team members trust one another enough to be able to disagree and argue about decisions and issues without it being personal; the focus is doing the right thing, discovering the truth, not winning an argument.

Buy-in

There is genuine buy-in and a strong sense of commitment from all team members when key decisions are taken, even if there has been earlier disagreement, because all ideas and views have been properly considered.

Performance

Team members, not just the leader, do not hesitate to hold one another to account for their behaviours and adherence to decisions and standards; there is a shared sense of ownership of the whole team's goals; the team is acting as a single unit and performing highly.

Having a framework can really help a team reflect on how it works together. In the day-to-day pressures of leading in a school, teams can be forgiven for sometimes finding it hard to find time to review strategic goals and progress towards them. It is even harder to devote valuable time to step back and reflect on how well your team is actually functioning. Yet, if Henry Ford is right, doing so is critical. To be moving forward together effectively, the senior team needs to be working in a way that harnesses the strengths and talents of everyone in the team and challenges itself to be even better.

And just as with a Model-T Ford, there need to be periodic checks of all the vital components. The Ford's oil filter and brake pads need renewing from time to time. Senior teams are no different. They can benefit from a simple diagnostic check and, just like cars, can benefit from the renewal of some of the basic elements that ensure smooth running. Using a model of team development can be one useful way of diagnosing how well your team is working. But finding time to use this analysis to then improve upon ways of working as well as recharging team relationships out of the work environment is also important.

Delegation

The job of any school leader is never done. Your to-do list just seems to keep getting longer. The scale of the pressures and expectations never seem to diminish. And of course one can add to that the pressure you usually place yourself under to do everything to a high standard, on time, and in a way that makes the biggest difference for your pupils.

There are no easy answers to resolving some of these tensions. However, the effective use of delegation can not only help you solve some of the pressures that you find yourself under, it can also empower, enable and support members of your team to develop or take their next professional step. When done well, delegation is a virtuous circle where all parties feel engaged, trusted and have a reasonably decent work-life balance.

Making delegation work

It isn't easy. When it comes to giving someone else in your team responsibility for writing a particular scheme of work, for example, or leading on a whole-school attendance initiative, there's always that nagging doubt in the back of your mind that you could probably do the job quicker and better than the person you are thinking of delegating to! On the other hand, failing to delegate effectively to members of your team can leave your staff with the feeling that they're given insufficient responsibility or that when they are, your inability to resist the temptation to micromanage makes them feel undervalued and distrusted.

There is another challenge that needs to be carefully considered. Leaders that delegate frequently can run the risk of being perceived to have abdicated their responsibilities. They are seen as simply passing jobs on just to get them off their desk. So it's important to make sure that when you delegate, others do not have that sense of abdication, but instead feel empowered and trusted.

So what makes for effective delegation?

First of all, you need to always consider what you're delegating and why you're delegating it. Are you delegating to get rid of work you just don't like or to develop someone?

Secondly, to be a good delegator you need to be able to let go. You just can't continue to control everything. You should hand over those tasks to other people that are stopping you from reaching your full potential because you're trying to do too much. The model below/overleaf from The Hay Group (2007) shows the three elements that need to be in place for successful delegation.

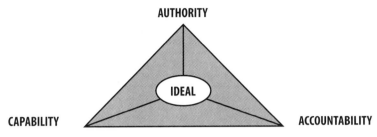

Figure 19: The three key elements needed for delegation
Hay Group

People can be most effective as leaders, and are most likely to take responsibility, when three things are in place:

- They have the *capability* they need, which includes skills and resources;
- They have the *authority* to act, to be an acknowledged decision maker in that field;
- They are also *accountable* for acting.

Providing two out of three is not enough, however:

- Accountability and authority without capability leaves a leader exposed, unable to do what is expected of them;
- Capability and accountability without authority leaves a leader undermined, constantly second-guessed and over-ruled;
- Capability and authority without accountability means the leader is sheltered from responsibility, which is potentially bad for the organisation.

It can often be useful to create a delegation plan. Some people find it helpful to create a matrix that shows members of a team, the main things the team is trying to achieve and the skills and experience each individual is gaining. Through this transparent approach, you will be showing the whole team that they are keen to both enable a fair and even distribution of responsibilities and ensure that each of them has a chance to take on new challenges and develop professionally.

Making sure that you have a good process of delegation is also very important. You first of all need to be clear that a particular task is suitable for delegation and that it can be successfully achieved by the person that you're delegating to. It is completely counter-productive for you to either delegate a task that in reality does need your input, or that is beyond the current capabilities and skills of the person you're attempting to delegate to. In either case, to delegate such a task is unfair on your team member will probably cause you more work in the long run.

Linked to this, it's really important to be clear what the task is that is being delegated and what is in scope and what isn't. People like to have clarity about what's expected of them so they can do a good job and not disappoint.

Linking delegation to performance development can also be very powerful. If, in discussions with your team, you are able to identify a particular development area for each team member, you have a very positive way into delegating tasks that will help those individuals build the skills and experience they are seeking to develop. As the earlier chapter on alignment pointed out, when it comes to motivating and influencing others, it's really important for you to put yourself in the position of the other person and understand their internal motivations and personal drivers. If when delegating, you're able to align what you need to have done with what people are looking to develop, you have created the classic win-win situation. That is why looking at delegation in the round and considering the needs of all of your team when drawing up your delegation plan has such potential. Working in this way, you are able to create the best fit across the whole of your team.

Also linked to developing the performance of your team is making sure that, together, you take time to identify any particular training needs. If you're asking one of the team, for example, to take a lead on data across the team or at a whole-school level, then it may well be the case that some training in the use of data or the software systems used in your school will be really helpful.

You might also want to consider providing coaching or mentoring support for members of your team. This could be provided by other members of the team, from elsewhere in the school or even from beyond the school. However this is achieved, when individuals are taking on new challenges, it can be really helpful to have the support and guidance of someone who is not part of the direct line management chain to help them get to grips with the new challenges they are facing.

A framework for delegation

When delegating tasks, it's also important to be flexible about how the delegation will work in practice. In this context it can be very helpful to use a delegation framework to identify the precise degree to which you are delegating. For example, when taking a decision, does someone you're delegating to (i) need to ask you for permission, (ii) ask for your advice and then decide or (iii) just tell you what they have done after the event?

There is a very simple framework that describes nine clear levels of delegation where level one represents no delegation whatsoever and level nine is, in effect, fully distributed leadership.

1. Look into this problem. Give me all the facts. I will decide what to do.
2. Let me know the alternatives available, with the pros and cons of each. I will decide what to select.
3. Let me know the criteria for your recommendation, which alternatives you have identified and which one appears best to you, with any risk identified. I will make the decision.
4. Recommend a course of action for my approval.
5. Let me know what you intend to do. Delay action until I approve.
6. Let me know what you intend to do. Do it unless I say not to.
7. Take action. Let me know what you did. Let me know how it turns out.
8. Take action. Communicate with me only if your action is unsuccessful.
9. Take action. No further communication with me is necessary.

Figure 20: The nine levels of delegation
Tim Brighouse (2007)

This framework can be a very useful way of agreeing with a member of any team where on the continuum you and your colleagues would like to operate. Of course, the further down the continuum one moves, the greater the degree of trust one needs to show in a team member, and the greater the degree of confidence they need to have in themselves to complete the delegated task or role successfully.

As part of agreeing a delegated task or role, it's important to reach agreement on the timeline and any deadlines. You also need to agree how you will know how well the project is progressing. Once this has been done, it can be quite useful to ask the team member to briefly write up what they think has been delegated, how they will take decisions and when they will report back. This is a really helpful way of both empowering them to own the task and giving you the opportunity to check that they have a shared understanding of what has been agreed.

Finally, it is really important for you to let people know how they are doing and if they are achieving their goal. If there are problems, you should try to avoid going into blame mode. Rather, identify what's gone wrong, try to understand together how this has happened and, ideally in a coaching conversation, help the team member to work out what needs to be done differently. That way, the team member continues to feel trusted but at the same time can learn from their experience and improve on their work. It is your responsibility, as the team leader, to absorb the consequences of failure and create the culture where setbacks are an opportunity to learn and grow.

1. When you delegate, make sure the other person is **set up to succeed** because they have the capacity and competence (with support, if needed) to achieve the task.

2. Make sure there is **clarity** about what is required, by when and to what standard. People usually don't know all the detail you have in your head.

3. **Be patient**. Remember that to start with it is unlikely that the person you are delegating to will carry out the task as well or as fast as you would.

4. Don't assume how much the person wants you to keep close to the task. Have a conversation. This will avoid them thinking you are either micro-managing or, at the other extreme, that you have abdicated your responsibility. **Agree with them** the frequency and nature of check-in points.

5. **Don't underestimate** what people are keen or able to take on. Usually people are pleased to be asked, especially if you are playing to people's strengths or stretching them.

6. Make sure the people you delegate to have the **authority and resource** to get the job done. And don't just delegate all the **boring jobs** or those you'd rather not do.

7. Make sure you **plan ahead** and give people plenty of time, rather than using delegation only when you are under pressure for time yourself.

8. Make sure you **don't delegate high risk or critical projects** unless you are

100% sure the person can deliver them. It isn't fair to put someone under that pressure.

9. When you delegate, think about **who else can help** or what the interdependencies of the work might be. Might it be something to delegate to a team rather than a person?

10. Make sure you say **thanks** for a job well done!

Figure 21: Top tips for effective delegation

And when success has been achieved, don't forget how important it is to properly credit whoever is responsible. However you do it, it's really important you pass on the credit for success, rather than let others think you have been responsible. Nothing is more dispiriting than for a team to see you take the credit for something you didn't do!

Summary

- What could you do to improve your team meetings?

- How could collaboration and team working be improved in your team?

- Would it be useful to use a framework to evaluate how well your team is working?

- Are there any steps you might take to delegate more effectively?

- Would it be useful to use the levels of delegation framework to help promote better delegation?

Chapter Eleven

Driving delivery

*However beautiful the strategy, you should
occasionally look at the results.*
Winston Churchill

When it comes to the key actions leaders need to undertake, we have so far focused on strategy, alignment, building relationships and creating great teams. All of these are clearly important. But in the end if, as a leader, you don't actually make anything happen, you won't deliver on your objectives.

From my experience, school leaders are very good at making things happen. The problem is, we have a tendency to take on too much ourselves and don't actually spend enough time on strategy and delivery through others. But that said, having worked with hundreds of school leaders, I do think there are some key things you can focus on. A number of these emerged from our G2G work in London. In particular, we concluded that it was critical for leaders to focus on the recruitment of high quality staff, the retention of those who have the biggest impact and the removal of those who fail to make the grade.

In his book *Good to Great*, Jim Collins (2001) uses the analogy of a bus to make this point. In this context, one of the most important things highly successful organisations do is get the right people on the bus, the wrong people off the bus, everyone in the right seats, and make sure the driver knows where the bus is headed. Of course, this particular analysis was originally based upon research in the business world and some heads have suggested that applying such principles in a school context is unrealistic, particularly as they perceive it is more difficult to tackle underperformance. Yet this is exactly what great schools do.

Recruitment

Care and attention is paid to each school's recruitment process. Advertisements are attractive, the interview is thorough and professional, and schools are not afraid to take the decision not to appoint and start over again if a suitable candidate fails to materialise. The more successful the school becomes, the easier it gets and the higher the bar can be raised. Increasingly, great schools and their governing bodies are using professional recruitment services, particularly for more senior appointments.

As Tim Brighouse and David Woods (2008) helpfully point out in *What makes a good school now?* being fussy about appointments is essential, no matter how challenging your recruitment context. They remind us that to 'appoint in haste, or when not entirely sure, is to repent at leisure'.

By the same token, you may need to be prepared to take a risk by overstaffing if a particular recruitment process produces two outstanding candidates for a post. Clearly financial constraints mean this is not possible in all circumstances, but in core subjects particularly, there is evidence to show this approach pays dividends in the longer term.

When one of the primary schools I used to work with needed to appoint an assistant headteacher, the candidates that were finally short-listed were all so good that the school appointed all three, despite the short term impact on the budget. As a result, the school had three excellent class teachers as well as three highly effective senior leaders who worked together to help the school become outstanding.

Another school appointed three very suitable PE candidates when only one permanent post was available. The skills set and attitude of the individuals was such that they adapted and were supported to be highly successful in alternative shortage fields. The school then supported those colleagues in taking the step back into their area of specialism when the right time came.

Thinking back to what builds discretionary effort, staff appointed need to fit with your school or group's core values. The recruitment process needs to assess whether the person is aware of the vision and shares in the values that underpin your work and has a genuine passion for the job on offer. One school we heard from asks potential candidates to read the school's pedagogical summary online and then asks questions at interview based on the document. Such an approach not only tests their understanding of good teaching but also says something about their self-motivation, organisational skills and how much they want to work in *your* school.

If you want to delegate to others more, you need to have people who are able to work without being tightly managed and whilst they may need to be guided, led and taught and do not need constant supervision. If too much time is spent on motivating and monitoring a colleague, the situation rapidly becomes mutually unproductive. The right people will be largely self-motivating and self-disciplined, compulsively driven to do the best they can.

Effective colleagues will also demonstrate a genuinely mature team approach to their work. For example when things are going well they will identify those people who have contributed to that success. When there has been a problem they will take responsibility rather than blame others.

The very best schools also take time to consider what balance is needed within any given team. One of the outstanding schools I have worked with uses the *StrengthsFinder* system when appointing staff. As well as watching teachers teach as part of the recruitment process, they ask prospective staff to undertake a *StrengthsFinder* questionnaire to better understand what individuals have to offer and how they will complement the needs of a particular team. They then use this knowledge to ensure that staff are given roles which play to their strengths. Using this approach has also given the school a common language when discussing the strengths or weaknesses of its work.

Retention

To retain good staff, it is important to make sure achievements are recognised, that working conditions are good, that staff can see progression in their career and that staffing structures are flexible enough to allow this to happen. More generally, there is no substitute for making sure that everything comes together to create the ethos of the school as positive and energetic. People like to work in a place that feels good about itself.

Indeed, such schools tend to have a generally more stable staff, running contrary to the common view that a good turnover of staff is necessary to bring in new experience and to provide opportunities for professional development.

As Peter Matthews in his Ofsted publication *Twelve outstanding secondary schools* (2009) points out, if teachers are good then heads will seek to retain them by providing new challenges, responsibilities and experience within the same school.

This lower staff turnover means it is easier for schools to maintain consistency in the way procedures and systems are followed. It also helps to foster strong relationships between the staff and pupils and promotes the previously mentioned strong team-based approach to embedding the deep-rooted culture within a school.

One head I know believes the school's low staff turnover is because of the in-house professional development and the opportunities provided for staff to take on temporary responsibilities. The school has developed its own web-based 'me and my career' model for staff, which suggests both activities and training at each stage in a teacher's career. Staff can complete the activities at their own pace and are then well placed for promotion.

Developing your staff

What is clear about all highly successful organisations, whether they are schools or businesses, is the fact that they share a strong commitment to enabling all members of staff, at all levels of the organisation, to develop as professionals and thereby continually improve their performance.

However, as we listened to the stories of some of our most successful schools in London, it became clear that this process was far more than just a mechanical continuing professional development system linked to performance management and personal target setting. These schools had an organic sense of self-improvement fuelled by the genuine and self-motivated desire of all the individuals to make things better.

Jim Collins (2012) identified a key similarity in all the organisations: a highly disciplined workforce. By this he didn't mean that there were strong command and control mechanisms operating. Rather, quite the reverse was true. Staff were highly focused around achieving their organisation's goals and were very self-motivated in trying to achieve them.

In our most successful schools the same is true. The staff strongly believe in acting in a collaborative way, reinforcing and emphasising a shared set of expectations and procedures. This self-discipline is not borne of a fear of failing to follow the rules but arises out of a strong acceptance and understanding of the principles underpinning each school's success.

This notion is perhaps best illustrated by reference to an everyday challenge in many secondary schools: how to manage the behaviour of pupils in the corridor? The answer on one level appears very simple: it is the responsibility of all staff to both challenge unacceptable behaviour when they come across it and to model appropriate behaviour. Of course the reality is that in many schools some staff will and some staff won't respond appropriately. In our best schools, so strong is the shared sense of ownership of standards and expectations that no matter which member of staff comes across a pupil running in the corridor, one can be almost 100% certain that the matter will be dealt with appropriately.

Gaining such consistency of approach cannot be arrived at by monitoring or checking; nor is it usually the subject of a performance review target. It stems from a sense of pride and caring as part of a collaborative team dedicated and committed to a genuinely shared set of goals.

This sense of pride takes time to develop and is the result of a lot of hard work and resilience on the part of school leaders over a significant period of time.

Learning in the workplace

When thinking about professional development in its widest sense, what has also become strongly evident is that the learning in the workplace is the most effective form of school improvement. And, of course, our best learning comes from when we make mistakes. So it follows that the best schools will have encouraged a climate where risk taking and innovation are part of the everyday culture. Teachers and support staff in great schools are constantly trying new ideas and experimenting with the way they do things. This naturally leads them to reflect upon their own best practice that leads to improved performance.

This can, of course, only happen in a school where making mistakes is seen as part of the process and not a reason to lay blame on someone. What was very evident in hearing about best practice at many of the schools who have presented at our termly conferences has been how new ideas and innovation did not arise in their final form when they were first tried. Several iterations were often necessary before something was fit for purpose. Peter Matthews, in his Ofsted publication, found that not only do the best schools have a systematic and finely tuned system of planning performance management and professional development, they also link this with a culture of sharing best practice within each institution through regular coaching, mentoring and self-evaluation.

Setting aside quality time to reflect on performance and to talk through challenges with someone who has good coaching skills can make a real difference. In the wider context, this approach is strongly validated by Daniel Goleman (2002), whose work in which he recognises the short term benefits of professional training, but advocates an approach based on ongoing workplace reflection and self-directed learning which he suggests has far greater long term impact. In these circumstances staff take on their own learning agenda almost in spite of, rather than because of, traditional performance management processes. This is not to under-estimate the crucial role such systems play. It's just that the highest performing institutions and schools are working at the next level where self-discipline and self-directed learning is at the heart of collective success.

1. Duration and rhythm of effective CPD support requires a longer-term focus. At least two terms to a year or longer is most effective, with follow up, consolidation and support activities built in.

2. Participants' needs should be carefully considered. This requires stepping away from a 'one size fits all' approach and creating content for teachers that integrates their day-to-day experiences and aspirations for their pupils with a shared and powerful sense of purpose.

3. Alignment of professional development processes, content and activities: ensuring there is a logical thread between the various components of the programme and creating opportunities for teacher learning that are consistent.

4. The content of effective professional development should consider both subject knowledge and subject-specific pedagogy in order to achieve the full potential of CPD, with clarity around learners' progress. In addition, content and activities should help teachers understand how pupils learn, both generally and in specific subject areas.

5. Effective professional development is associated with certain activities. These include explicit discussions, experimenting and testing ideas in the classroom and analysis of, and reflection around, the evidence and relevant assessment data.

6. External input from providers and specialists must challenge orthodoxies within a school and provide multiple, diverse perspectives. Facilitators acting as coaches and/or mentors should provide support through modelling, observation and feedback.

7. Empowering teachers through collaboration and peer learning: teachers should have opportunities to work together, try out and refine new approaches and tackle teaching and learning challenges.

8. Powerful leadership around professional development is pivotal in defining staff opportunities and embedding cultural change. School leaders should not leave the learning to teachers, they should be actively involved themselves.

Figure 22: What makes good CPD?
Adapted from a publication commissioned by the Teacher Development Trust from Durham University, Curee and UCL IoE.

One school has weekly optional training for all staff and these sessions are very well attended. The staff leading the programme take suggestions on what to include and believe the high levels of attendance reflect the fact that what is on offer is tailored to what staff have said they are interested in. Rather than plan and publish in advance, the sessions are reactive and specific to immediate demand from staff. The topic will be announced each week and include examples such as: great group work, creating independence and positive relationship promotion.

As well as asking the staff for suggestions, the senior team also identifies need and excellent practice whilst on daily learning walks and the staff themselves are encouraged to present at the weekly training sessions. In this way, all staff are given the opportunity to play a part in the development of others.

Incremental coaching

In the last few years I have become increasingly convinced that a powerful way to support teachers' development and improve the quality of teaching is to use regular 'incremental' coaching. I first came across this approach in Paul Bambrick-Santoyo's (2012) *Leverage Leadership*.

His approach is based on avoiding some of the common errors he believes we make when thinking about how best to improve the performance of teachers. These are set out in figure 23 below.

Error 1: More is better.

Top-tier Truth: Less is more. Many leaders fall prey to the temptation to deliver feedback on every aspect of the lesson. While that is a useful tool to demonstrate your instructional expertise, it won't change practice nearly as effectively. As we can learn from coaches in every field, bite-sized feedback on just one or two areas delivers the most effective improvement

Error 2: Lengthy written evaluations drive change as effectively as any other form of feedback.

Top-tier Truth: Face-to-face makes the difference. The reason why this error persists nationwide among school leaders is that there is a subset of teachers for whom lengthy written evaluations are effective (just like there is a small group of learners for whom lengthy lectures are most effective). This leads to the dangerous conclusion that all teachers develop well by reading lengthy evaluations In what other field do we subscribe to this idea?

Error 3: Just tell them; they'll get it.

Top-tier Truth: If they don't do the thinking, they won't internalise what they learn. In classroom instruction, highly effective teachers push the students to do the thinking. If teachers eclipse this thinking by providing conclusions or answers too quickly, students will disengage. Feedback is not any different: if teachers don't participate in the process of thinking about their teaching, they are less likely to internalise the feedback. This is metacognition applied to teacher development: having teachers think about their teaching improves their performance.

Error 4: State the concrete action step. Then the teacher will act.

Top-tier Truth: Guided practice makes perfect. If a surgeon simply tells a resident how to perform an operation, the resident will be less effective than if she practices with the surgeon's guidance. Teaching is the same: practicing implementation of the feedback with the *leader* is at the heart of speeding up the improvement cycle. It also allows teachers to make mistakes before they're in front of the students again.

Error 5: Teachers can implement feedback at any time.

Top-tier Truth: Nail down the timing. Having a concrete timeline in which feedback will be implemented serves two purposes: it makes sure everyone has clear expectations as to when this will be accomplished and it will expose action steps that are not really able to be accomplished in a week.

Figure 23: Five errors to avoid when it comes to helping teachers improve

Adapted from *Leverage Leadership*, by Paul Bambrick-Santoyo (2012)

Incremental coaching adopts an approach that is designed to avoid these shortcomings. It typically involves a short drop-in to a lesson where the short coaching conversation that follows, ideally that day, elicits the areas of strength and a single area of focus for improvement with some strategies to try. Ideally, the teacher has a chance to practise these as part of the follow-up conversation. The teacher then spends just one week really focusing on this single area for improvement until the next short drop-in a week later when there can then be a discussion about the progress that has been made. This may result in another week or two on the same focus or the opportunity to move into a new area. As the model below suggests, questioning starts very open, allowing the teacher to work out as much as possible for themselves. Only if needed are more closed or probing questions introduced. In all cases, clear actions for follow-up are clarified, with a clear timeline for each.

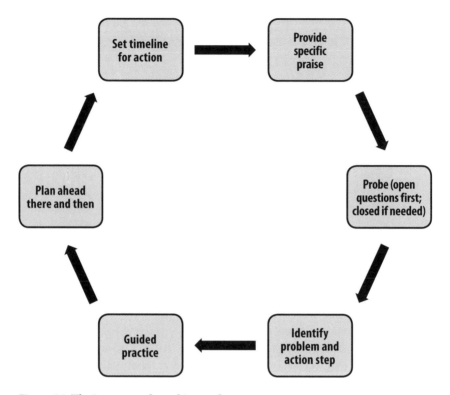

Figure 24: The incremental coaching cycle
Adapted from *Leverage Leadership*, by Paul Bambrick-Santoyo (2012)

Over time, this incremental process enables teachers to develop mastery in the full range of basic classroom skills and pedagogies that will lead to improved classroom delivery and improved outcomes for pupils. At its heart, the incremental coaching approach gives ownership for improvement to the teachers themselves.

Developing leadership talent

Within the wider context of developing your staff, another thing that great schools are good at is identifying and nurturing talent. Whatever level of leadership you are currently working at, you have the opportunity to spot the future middle and senior leaders in those you are working with. Apart from the obvious benefits for succession planning within your own school or group of schools, we all have a responsibility to develop the pipeline of school leaders across the country. Great schools have systematic programmes of leadership development in place to do just this. As well as opportunities for learning about leadership in theory, critical elements of these programmes include the chance to take on new roles and experiences, work-shadow and have coach/mentor support. I have worked within a number of groups of schools to help them do just this across more than one school, which opens up a whole range of other exciting opportunities.

But there are some things we need to be better at in this regard. I still don't think we are good enough at recognising the inherent unconscious bias we all have, myself included, that tends to see 'potential' as looking like us! By recruiting and developing staff according to the norms that already exist, we run the risk that future leaders will continue to be dominated by white males who may, some would argue, have a tendency to lead in a certain way. When I talk about knowing and understanding the strengths and talents of others in your team in chapter 5, it is important to remember that different leaders bring different strengths. Not everyone should conform to a certain view of what a leader 'looks like'. In one school's senior leadership team with whom I worked recently, and where the head had been in place for a number of years and had appointed pretty much the whole team, 90% of his colleagues had identical personality profiles. He had appointed in his own image!

We also need to make it easier for women in particular (but not exclusively), to combine the challenges and pressures of working as a school leader with family life. Again, this requires heads and system leaders to think more creatively and differently about how they can be more flexible in the way things are organised within schools.

Lateral leadership

This sense of the ownership of learning is also key to what Michael Fullan (2007) describes as lateral leadership. For many years the debate around school improvement has included a discussion about whether a top-down or bottom-up approach brings the greatest level of success. Early on it was clear that top-down approaches on their own don't work. While there was clear evidence that in many circumstances bottom-up improvement was more successful, the results are inevitably inconsistent, with some areas both within and between schools failing to reach acceptable standards of performance.

The concept of lateral leadership is based on peer-to-peer support, either within a single school context or between two or more schools working together. With a growing number of teaching school alliances and academy trusts complementing pre-existing networks, there are many opportunities for this type of collaboration. Often based around a coaching model, the approach allows for individuals to take responsibility for their own learning whilst at the same time having appropriate levels of challenge from a professional colleague. This approach is not limited to senior or middle leaders but can be applied at all levels within the teaching and support staff of any school.

One school I know has worked hard to create a climate where risk taking is encouraged. Great lessons are photographed, described and shared via Twitter or whole-staff emails. There are signs used saying 'I am taking a risk' which can go on classroom doors if staff are being extra-creative and worried whether an approach will work or not. The most effective teachers are trained as peer coaches and the school uses 'learning three' teams as part of its teacher development programme for newly qualified staff. These teams consist of one teacher in their first, second and third year of teaching. Many schools, building on the concept of working in threes, are now using a 'lesson study' approach to professional development.

Key to the success of any self-improvement, particularly in the context of lateral leadership, is the notion of appreciative enquiry. The best schools take the view that it is always better to build on perceived and actual strengths than simply concentrate on the problems that need solving. This approach recognises that creating an environment where it is okay to try out new ideas needs to be based on a credit, not deficit, model of school improvement.

One word of caution. Schools need to be rigorous in the way they define outstanding practice before they share it. Too often, one can fall into the trap of recycling mediocre practice rather than genuinely effective and innovative ways of working. To do this requires a culture of honest feedback where the trust between individuals and schools enables this to happen and where taking an evidence-based approach, as we discussed previously, is at the heart of your strategy.

Holding to account

Accountability isn't always perceived as a positive thing but in the long-term it really does make everyone's job easier and a school better. Schools with clear accountability structures, systems and cycles, with excellent quality assurance at every level, achieve great things. The structure has to be fair, mutually agreed, understood and consistent to achieve optimum impact. Being held to account, when it is done well, should feel like a positive and rewarding experience. From the perspective of one of your teachers, for example, it is the feeling that you are clear about your role and responsibilities; you have been challenged by the requirements but have support in place if you need it. As you achieve benchmarks, you receive timely advice and constructive and helpful feedback and feel a sense of recognition and success when all has been achieved.

When accountability is used less wisely, it can create a fear factor in a school community. If people are less clear on their role or responsibility, they do not feel ownership, and are quick to blame others or cover up mistakes rather than be honest. Accountability at its best is constantly demanding the highest performance from every individual in the organisation. People know what their role looks like if it is done outstandingly well. If standards are not met, leaders are unafraid to look the person in the eye and say 'this is not good enough'. Swift intervention is undertaken and consequences enforced. How to approach these difficult conversations is described later in this chapter.

Systematising your processes can be really helpful. You should try to be specific about what will be reviewed and when. You need to specify who will deliver the data or evidence required and outline the criteria for how its impact will be measured. You should aim to provide people with a checklist of what should be achieved in a typical week, month, term or year for each role in their team.

In the case of exam results, checking performance on a pupil-by-pupil basis is essential for good accountability. With this in place, how do you measure interim progress? What checks will you put in place to reassure yourself that you are on target and at which point should interventions, if necessary as a last resort, be put in place? A calendar and list of checkpoints should be shared with the success criteria clearly articulated, very similar to a mark scheme. This is a transparent and shared way of measuring success. At a whole-school level, there may be a rhythm to this already established.

The least comfortable part of accountability is having difficult conversations. No one enjoys them. However there is a range of ways to deliver a difficult message. At worst, the outcome is 'lose-lose'; you feel awful and the recipient feels destroyed. At best, the outcome is a 'win-win'; you feel as though you could not have delivered the message in a better way; and the recipient feels clear on their next actions and as though they have been treated fairly.

For a 'win-win' scenario, you need to think through what you want to say and the message that needs to be relayed. Practise it so that your words are clear (nothing worse than you thinking you have said it gently and them completely missing the point and carrying on with the behaviour!) Make it short; the minute you carry on speaking, you muddle the message and talk yourself back out of it.

Putting off conversations you dread usually only makes them worse. But once you have had a few (conversations, not glasses of wine!), they do get easier. If you are about to have a difficult conversation, Susan Scott (2003), who is well known for her work in this area, recommends covering the following in that start to the conversation, uninterrupted:

1. Name the issue;

2. Describe a specific Example;

3. Describe your Feelings about the issue;

4. Clarify what is at stake, why this is Important;

5. Accept your contribution to this problem;

6. Indicate your wish to Resolve the issue;

7. Invite Them to respond.

The highlighted letters in the list above can be an easy way for your middle leaders to remember the seven steps as they form the acronym NEFI ART. Critical in the process is making sure that once the situation has been set out that you do not go on to try to solve the issue until you have an acceptance from the other person of the validity of the concern.

This all sounds fine in theory, but you need to make sure that not only have you properly prepared to give this introduction, but that you have also considered what may follow. There may be a whole range of responses, from silence or anger to complete denial or emotional collapse. Thinking through in advance how you might respond to each of these can be helpful.

You also need to try not to fall into the trap of 'propping up' the discussion that follows. Use questions to get the other person to talk and reflect on the issue, gain understanding and give a commitment to action. Let silences happen rather than being tempted to fill them. As Susan Scott suggests, let the silence do the heavy lifting. If the discussion goes off track, bring the dialogue back onto the issue they raised at the start.

You need to keep in mind your overall approach to managing the issue. Remember that in relation to Kilmann's (1994) model from earlier, in having a difficult conversation you are in 'forcing', 'collaborating' or 'compromising' mode. You are not smoothing or avoiding. This can be particularly important if you know you have a tendency to gloss over issues in the hope that they will go away or be tackled another time. You need to be disciplined. You also need to manage your own emotions, keeping to the facts at hand and the issue of concern.

If the conversation has gone well, the other person will not only have clarity about the issue, they will often feel relieved that it is out in the open and that a way forward has been agreed. You will usually go away feeling relieved that you have done the hardest part. But making sure you monitor the follow-up is critical.

Such discussions are serious, professional conversations. You cannot rely on or expect an existing friendship, personal loyalty or how long you have known and worked with someone to get you through such a meeting. Likewise, however, you can't suddenly turn on 'seniority' mode and pull rank just to get your point across on a one-off occasion. Be empathetic, understanding and listen. Treat the recipient as you would wish to be treated if this were *your* line manager talking to you.

Allow the person to respond and, out of fairness, listen to what they say, but agree the issue and clear action points on what needs to happen. Finish with checking that they feel that they have been treated fairly. Where appropriate, clarify the action points in writing. It is important that the written part is supportive rather than seen as 'I am putting this in writing', which has different connotations. If the recipient feels that you have been fair, feels that what has been said is true, has a clear idea of how to respond and deliver and then does so, then you have had a 'win-win'.

Moving people on

For most staff, even when performance drops, a good conversation and some high quality support can get a situation back on track. But there will sometimes be times when you need to be clear about moving someone on when it is obvious they are not performing. All schools are required to have disciplinary and competency procedures, but in some they remain an underused vehicle for creating and maintaining high standards. There is nothing more frustrating for the hard-working and capable majority than to see a colleague who is not able or not interested in delivering to the desired standards being allowed to carry on unchallenged. Inevitably, if this situation is allowed to continue, other colleagues may start to become demotivated and their own standards will also quickly begin to drop.

Of course, all colleagues are entitled to an appropriate level of confidentiality in such situations, but the staff as a whole is usually very quick to recognise when action has been taken to deal with underperformance of a particular individual, and this can be a powerful motivator amongst the wider staff body who do see it as the role of leaders to ensure everyone on the team is delivering.

Over time, the culture in a school can change dramatically. As one of the outstanding schools I have worked with describes, 'we have become increasingly confident in supportively yet assertively setting clear expectations for underperforming colleagues. Without ever needing to publicise the fact, other colleagues recognise that this is happening and see it as a positive rather than a threatening aspect of our approach.'

How the very best schools go about addressing issues of underperformance varies from school to school and from individual case to individual case. In some schools where a culture of high expectations is well established, simply beginning a competency procedure with a member of staff can often be sufficient for them to take the decision to move on. The profession faces, however, a wider problem of how to prevent the recycling of such poor performers from one school to another, a debate that probably extends beyond the scope of this book.

In other scenarios, particularly where a member of staff may have given long service to the school, schools often have a more informal conversation around the particular circumstances of that individual's career stage. Increasingly, this may involve reaching an agreed financial settlement.

Back me or sack me

In all cases, however, what all leaders should do is ensure that individuals that need it are offered 100% support in the first instance. Only if the required improvements fail to take place does it become necessary to consider the alternatives. This will involve working out an appropriate exit strategy and keeping to it.

The best schools have real clarity about where they are in the process and avoid vacillating between trying to support and trying to move someone on. When all else has failed, they take decisive action and relentlessly pursue the goal to move someone on. This 'back me or sack me' approach sounds somewhat draconian, but it is really important to be clear about where you are in tackling an individual's underperformance.

In schools where support is provided without clear targets and where a set period for performance review is not established, my own experience suggests this lack of clarity can lead to the failure to take decisive action to remedy the situation. Underperformance can go on for long periods where a school recognises the problem but almost unconsciously accepts it. Our pupils deserve better than this. They only have one chance.

Building momentum

In his book *Good to Great*, Jim Collins (2001) describes what he calls the 'flywheel concept'. He asks the reader to consider how a typical flywheel works. The principal aim is to store energy and build momentum. Pushing a heavy cast-iron disc is incredibly difficult in the early stages and progress appears slow. Gradually, over time, with a concerted and sustained effort, the flywheel will build its momentum. As more and more people join in pushing the flywheel so its speed will grow and grow until eventually everyone could let go and the flywheel would continue unimpeded.

The analogy works in schools as well as in business. People instinctively want to join something that is building and growing. The fact that the departure of a key leader or other individuals does not mean the flywheel stops also effectively illustrates the importance of a whole organisation developing its own momentum rather than the alternative approach where the success of a school is dependent upon a single person or small group of people.

Reflecting on the leadership model that underpins this book, the flywheel analogy also reinforces the importance of alignment. If some people were pushing the flywheel in the opposite direction it would clearly not gain momentum. Everyone needs to be pushing in the same direction if success is to be achieved.

This idea of gradually building performance and delivery over time, with a focus on incremental improvement, underpins the concept of building *marginal gains*. This approach has underpinned the success of the British cycling team which has concentrated on executing small changes really well. The combined impact of these changes has made them world class. The team, led by Dave Brailsford, believed that it is easier to make ten 1% improvements than it is to make one 10% change. This concept is, of course, at the heart of the incremental coaching approach mentioned earlier in this chapter.

Momentum brings resilience and strength in depth

There are times when schools encounter difficulties. In these circumstances the energy that the workforce as a whole is able to apply may diminish on a temporary basis. But where, as a leader, you have built strength in depth, where momentum and direction of travel has been clearly established, you are able to ride through temporary difficulty. The built-up momentum carries you through. If, for example, a key member of staff leaves your team, such is the shared way of working and the clear understanding of the 'way we do things around here' that the team can absorb the temporary blip. No one is suggesting that maintaining high performance in schools is easy, but what does seem to help is strength in depth built up over a number of years.

The best schools, therefore, are the result of a relentless and focused effort sustained over time where all stakeholders are consistently pushing in the same direction; they represent an aligned implementation of policy where success breeds success and where it becomes hard for everyone in the school to resist joining in and becoming part of that success.

Key points

- Are you rigorous in the processes you use to appoint staff and if you are in any doubt, you decide not to appoint?

- Do you sometimes take a risk when two exceptional candidates emerge for one appointment?

- Have you created a climate where opportunities for staff career development and progression are usually provided in-house?

- Do your staff want to improve for the sake of learning itself? Are you confident you are only sharing genuinely outstanding practice within school?

- Do you challenge under performance effectively through focused support and, if this is unsuccessful, do you have processes in place to swiftly move on underperforming staff?

- Do you have sufficient momentum that will help you through difficult periods?

Chapter Twelve

Planning and organisation

People don't resist change. They resist being changed.

Peter Senge

At its heart, the role of any leader is all about making change happen, not just for a while but for the long term. Whether that be improving the performance of a colleague in a particular area of practice, or designing and implementing a new policy or curriculum, the key to the success of any change is that it sticks. Too often in schools someone focuses on improving an area of practice, but not for long enough or in a sufficiently systematic way to ensure a change is embedded and will have a long-term impact on pupil outcomes.

Similarly, when it comes to developing a new policy or approach, an individual can sometimes introduce the new idea without properly engaging with those who will be responsible for making it happen or really thinking through how it will be implemented in practice. Before long the idea has withered on the vine or, at best, is being inconsistently applied.

So how do you approach changing things in a way that will bring about sustainable impact for your pupils? There are many theories about how to 'do' change. Many originate with leadership and change management guru, John Kotter. A professor at Harvard Business School and world-renowned change expert, Kotter (1996) introduced his eight-step change process in his book, *Leading Change* shown below.

Figure 25: *Eight steps of change*
John Kotter

Step one: increase urgency

For change to happen, it helps if the whole team or the school really wants it. So how do you engage staff when there is a natural resistance to change? How do you develop a sense of urgency around the need for change. This may help you spark the initial motivation to get things moving.

This isn't simply a matter of you showing staff a set of plateauing test results or scaring them about Ofsted, the demands of a new curriculum or an attendance target. It is about you instigating an open and honest and convincing dialogue about what's happening in the educational landscape and with your context. You might decide it would be useful to identify potential problems that lie ahead if they don't change, and develop scenarios showing what could happen in the future. However you achieve this, you need to start honest discussions and give dynamic and convincing reasons to get people talking and thinking.

Step two: build a 'change-team'

As with any whole school change, if time permits, it's a good idea to get a small group of people to work up your ideas. Using your change-team to help develop your plans is useful in itself. But having them as a small group of advocates for the rest of the team can be very powerful, particularly if they have managed to include one or two key influencers in your group.

If you are leading across more than one school, steps one and two in Kotter's model are particularly important if you are going to gain the traction you are likely to need.

Step three: get the vision right

When you first start thinking about change, there will probably be many great ideas and solutions floating around. You need to link these concepts to an overall vision that people can grasp easily and remember. A clear vision can help everyone understand why you're asking them to do something. When people see for themselves what you're trying to achieve, then the directives they're given tend to make more sense. Consulting on the vision for a change can also be a good way for you to help generate interest in making the change.

Step four: communication for buy-in

What you and your change-team do with your plans after they have been created is crucial. Your message will probably have strong competition from other day-to-day pressures and priorities, so you need to communicate it frequently and powerfully, and embed it within everything that you do. You need to keep telling the story.

Involving pupils and parents in this stage can be a powerful way of building buy-in for an idea. It also helps the staff see the benefits for the pupils in a way they may not have quite appreciated.

It's also important for you, as the driver of the change to 'walk the talk'. What you actually do is often far more important – and believable – than what you say. You should demonstrate the kind of behaviour that you want from others.

Step five: enable action

If you follow these steps and reach this point in the change process, you've been talking about the vision and building buy-in. Hopefully, staff want to get busy and achieve the benefits that you have been promoting.

But is anyone resisting the change? And are there processes or structures that are getting in its way? There is further guidance towards the end of this chapter about how you might approach this.

It's also important for you not to forget to identify and put in place the structure for change, and continually check for barriers to it. Removing obstacles can empower the people you need to execute the vision, and it can help the change move forward. One way to do this is to delegate to mini-teams. A great example here is on curriculum planning. Pairing up members of a team to devise a unit of work, where the pairings have been carefully thought through, can be a great way to remove obstacles to engagement in change. At a more senior level, using sub-teams to deliver on a change can be a great way of playing to strengths and keeping things manageable.

Step six: create short-term wins
Nothing motivates more than success. Look out for ways you can give your staff a taste of victory early in the change process. Within a short time frame they need to have results they can see. Without this, critics and negative thinkers might damage progress. People need to be thinking quickly that the change is a good thing – they need to 'feel the benefit' fast.

Step seven: don't let up
Kotter argues that many change projects fail because victory is declared too early. Real change runs deep. Quick wins are only the beginning of what needs to be done to achieve long-term change. In particular, you need to tackle those that don't appear to be on board with the change. Typically, these 'laggards' are the last to adopt any change. If you have spent time properly defining how the change will work at stage two and three, then these are easy conversations to have. There is nothing worse than saying to someone that they need to make a change when you know deep down it isn't 100% the right thing to be doing.

Each success you have also provides an opportunity to build on what went right and identify what can be improved. Make sure you take time to reflect, as a team, on 'what went well' and 'even better if.'

Step eight: make it stick

Finally, to make any change stick, it should become part of your culture. It should be consistently applied. A team's culture often determines what gets done, so the values behind the vision must show in day-to-day work.

Your systems for monitoring need to place a value on the things you have changed to help embed them. The key milestones should be part of the wider team or school's development plan. How you recognise and celebrate success, both as a school and as a team, also needs to reflect the changes you have made.

Managing the effect of change on others

People respond differently to change. But all of us, when there is a major change happening, tend to go through a series of stages of feelings about the change. This can also affect our own feelings of self-worth or competence. It is not uncommon for people to doubt they can perform successfully in the way a change may demand. The most commonly known model for illustrating how this happens was developed by Elisabeth Kübler-Ross (1969) and is shown in the diagram below/overleaf.

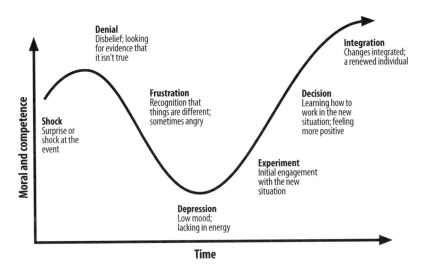

Figure 26: The change curve
Adapted from the Kübler-Ross model

When you are introducing a significant change, it is well worth taking some time out to think about how each of the individuals in the team are likely to react and then work out the best way to approach things with them, without compromising on your overall goals. As a school, you may wish to use one of the personality pre-disposition tools available, such as those we have developed at Leadership Matters, to support this. Once again, this is about understanding your situation before acting.

Final thoughts

In addition to (i) using Kotter's eight-step model as a useful guide to thinking about change and (ii) thinking about how different team members may respond to change, you may also want to consider these last four points:

- Keep the change you want to make as simple as possible. This makes it easier to communicate, easier to get buy-in, easier to deliver consistently and easier to monitor impact;

- When you consult on a particular change, you should remember to thank everyone who has taken the time to give you feedback and welcome their input, even though some of it may be negative. Giving people a proper chance to get things 'off their chest' can be an important part of the change process;

- After consultation, always make sure you feedback what you have heard. In particular, where you have decided not to act on a particular viewpoint, you should take the time to explain why. This is often best done face-to-face. It is important for people to feel they have been heard, even if, in the end, their argument hasn't won the day (from my experience, school leaders aren't good at this);

- You should be prepared to be flexible, but only if in doing so you can take more people with you and still make the change you want to make. Showing flexibility can also be important if the change you have made doesn't appear to have been successful. If, after a sufficient period of time, there is clear evidence that the whole team has worked hard for a change but it isn't delivering the impact you had hoped, it is a sign of strength to acknowledge this and find another way forward.

Using data to plan

As the old adage suggests, continually weighing a pig doesn't make it any fatter. That's the point made by critics who think that some schools spend too much time and energy measuring anything that moves at the expense of concentrating on ensuring lessons are well-planned, well-executed and fun for pupils. Indeed, there are schools that spend a lot of time collecting all kinds of data that have little impact on pupils' learning outcomes. Tables and tables of information sitting on a marvellous database does little in itself to drive up standards.

But farmers would argue otherwise. There will always be a need to weigh a pig from to time to time to make sure there is nothing wrong with it. It ought to be gaining weight at a certain rate – if it isn't, then why not? Monitoring the pig's weight allows the farmer to intervene if there is a problem. It allows the farmer to reflect on what works best and what doesn't seem to be working. It allows the farmer to try out new ideas and evaluate whether they are a success.

In other words, when it comes to data, you need to model your practice on the farming profession! You need to know how well pupils are progressing; they and your team need to have data that will help them reflect on what is working and what is not. They need to be able to intervene when an individual or a particular group of pupils appears to be falling behind. They also need to be able to see the overall 'big picture'. Are there changes that need to be made to the curriculum or to a particular scheme of work?

What is important here is the frequency and accuracy of data and the pupil-by-pupil analysis that leads to timely and focused planning. This can only happen if data is current and has been collected efficiently and accurately. Basing intervention on out-of-date data is a waste of everyone's time and will fail to secure buy-in from staff or pupils. Hopefully your whole-school systems will have all this in place. If colleagues are telling you otherwise, maybe it is time to look again at how you organise your data processes.

Whatever the practicalities of process, accuracy is critical. This means it is essential that you have robust systems for moderating pupils' achievements, both through work scrutiny and high quality testing. For middle leaders, in particular, regularly allocating time to this in meetings, where this is possible, is a really useful way of making sure everyone is working to the same set of expectations about what constitutes a particular grade or level. Some teams find it helpful to keep portfolios of work as part of the evidence that can support this approach.

I would offer one caveat here. Learning doesn't always happen in a linear way. All of us working in schools need to use our professional judgement to get the balance right between understanding precisely what pupils can and can't do rather than trying to define a broad level that they have reached. Some of the recent changes to assessments in England have been introduced with this in mind. Putting aside the way in which these changes have been introduced, the idea of 'best-fit' assessment when it comes to making formative judgements was a feature of previous assessment systems that wasn't really in pupils' interests.

As well as thinking about individual pupil progress and interventions, looking at the data from a curriculum point of view, by using question-level analysis, for example, is another powerful tool to raise standards. In any given area, is there a skill/content area in which pupils under-perform in a particular class or in all classes? Is there a subject knowledge gap within the teaching that needs to be addressed? Do boys perform better or worse than girls in a particular area?

The data should be used for effective conversations and comparisons around these types of questions within teams. All staff should feel a clear sense of accountability for the pupils in their care and be clear about their role in providing accurate and timely data and planning effective interventions. There should be a healthy balance between challenge and support for both pupils and staff. Linked to this, as mentioned already, it is important to ensure you build in formal opportunities to celebrate success and recognise achievements. Again, this applies equally to staff and pupils.

Using your resources wisely to deliver

There is never enough resource to do everything you would like to do. Budgets are always tight. Whether we are working in the public or private sector, there is a responsibility on all of us in education to make sure we are spending our limited resource to its best effect. This requires proper planning. It is also important for all leaders to ensure financial probity. Systems need to be in place to ensure that the purchasing of goods and services is carried out through due financial process and that any income generation is handled appropriately.

The resource planning cycle

At its simplest level, there are four key stages to the process of strategic resource planning. These can equally be applied to leaders at all levels:

1. Agreeing your overall strategic *aims*, including any new strategic priorities you wish to undertake;

2. Agreeing your strategic *plan*. This sets out how you plan to achieve your aims;

3. Working out the *cost* of the different elements of your strategic plan. This will include working out those on-going running costs that need to be covered as well as any start-up costs that may relate to new initiatives that you want to implement;

4. Ensuring you are getting the best *value-for-money* for your investment. This will require thinking carefully about how you procure goods or services as well as how you ensure you make efficient use of the resources at your disposal. More on this later.

There is a whole other language around resource management, some of which sounds far more complex than it actually is. You may well know what many of the terms below mean but just in case, here are a few definitions you may find helpful reminders.

Revenue and capital costs

Revenue costs are recurring costs, year on year. They include items like staffing, consumables and on-going replacement for items such as furniture. Capital expenditure is one-off spending on items that won't need replacing for some time, such as a new suite of computers, a new classroom or new furniture.

Economy

This refers to keeping costs as low as possible. It is about getting a good price for the items or services you are purchasing. Typically, researching the market and buying in bulk helps drive down costs and improve economy.

Efficiency

This refers to how you use what you have procured. You may have purchased a new microscope at a great price, but if it is hardly ever used, that is a very inefficient use of the resource. Likewise, expenditure on IT equipment and software that is used by the whole team, the whole time, is a very efficient use of resource.

Effectiveness

This relates to whether your spending gives good value for money. It isn't simply about how cheap something was to purchase or how well it is being used. It is the overall judgement about the impact of your spending in relation to what you are trying to achieve. Measuring effectiveness is much more difficult than measuring economy or efficiency, but it is ultimately the most important judgement to make. It is an old cliché, but the cheapest isn't always the best. What matters is delivering great value for money.

There has been a lot of research undertaken in recent years about the relative effectiveness of the different ways schools spend their money. The diagram below/overleaf sets out some of the key messages emerging from this research. Again, this is probably something you are already familiar with but is included here for completeness.

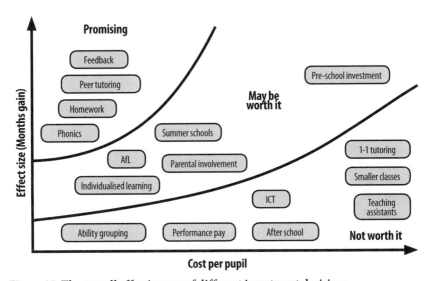

Figure 27: The overall effectiveness of different investment decisions

Adapted from Education Endowment Foundation (2013) Teaching and Learning Toolkit

You might be surprised to see the impact of smaller class sizes and the typical effectiveness of the use of teaching assistants or the use of 1:1 tuition. Of course, this research is based on the typical impact of these different approaches rather than what is the case in individual schools. But they give us all serious food for thought.

But as with all evidence, the important thing is to consider it within your context. As Dylan Wiliam says, "What works is not the right question. Everything works somewhere. Nothing works everywhere. What's interesting is under what conditions does this work?" The most recent research from the Education Endowment Fund (2015) on the effective use of teaching assistants is a case in point. Whilst the overall analysis for the impact of using TAs in the way they tend to be used suggests they represent poor value for money, but when used in the right way they can have significant impact. The table below summarises the key findings of this research.

1. TAs should not be used as an informal teaching resource for low-attaining pupils
2. Use TAs to add value to what teachers do, not replace them

3. Use TAs to help pupils develop independent learning skills and manage their own learning

4. Ensure TAs are fully prepared for their role in the classroom

5. Use TAs to deliver high-quality one-to-one and small group support using structured interventions

6. Adopt evidence-based interventions to support TAs in their small group and one-to-one instruction

7. Ensure explicit connections are made between learning from everyday classroom teaching and structured interventions

Figure 28: Making the most of teaching assistants: key recommendations

Adapted from Education Endowment Fund (2015)

Prioritising for impact

If there's one thing all school leaders have in common, it's the fact that it just seems like there's never enough time to do the job. Apart from managing the workload associated with your classes, including preparation and marking, there's everything you are accountable for in your leadership role. But have you ever stopped and really properly thought about what you do with your time, or thought about whether there are things you could do to ease the burden and make things more efficient?

Approaches to managing time

The reality is that people have very different approaches to the use of time. Some people are actually energised by deadlines and find it most productive to leave things to the last minute. Others can't bear the thought of having everything left until the last minute and will want everything planned out well in advance. Then there are those who just can't say 'no' when a job comes up. These are people who never stop to ask themselves whether they have time to do everything they have agreed to. Others are great procrastinators who will always find something else to do than the things they really should be doing. Finally, there are those who just have to spend the time to get the detail right, even if that means other things are delayed or stress levels rise.

You probably know leaders that fit all of these descriptions. You may also find it interesting to reflect on your own pre-dispositions in this respect! For all leaders, when it comes to better time management, knowing your own pre-dispositions can be helpful.

Urgent versus important

Regardless of your own approach to the use of time, there are some universal truths that are worth bearing in mind. In his book *The 7 Habits of Highly Effective People*, Steven Covey (2004) introduces the very helpful distinction between things that are urgent and things that are important. How often are you asked to do things urgently by someone else when you are not convinced about the need to do whatever you are being asked in the first place? Or how often do you prioritise some things over others as a way of avoiding the things you don't really want to do? The diagram below/overleaf sets this out.

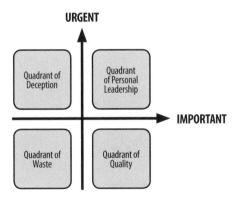

Figure 29: The four quadrants of time management
Adapted from a model by Stephen Covey (1990)

For each of the four quadrants, Covey suggests how you should respond. The last of these (sometimes referred to as quadrant two or Q2) is the most critical and the one middle leaders find the most difficult to do.

Urgent and important – do now

Subject to confirming the importance and the urgency of these tasks, do these tasks now. Prioritise according to their relative urgency.

Urgent but not important – reject and explain
Scrutinise and probe demands. Help originators to re-assess. Wherever possible reject and avoid these tasks sensitively and immediately.

Not urgent nor important – resist and cease
Habitual 'comforters' not true tasks. Non-productive, de-motivational. Minimise or cease altogether. Plan to avoid them.

Not urgent but important – plan to do
Critical to success: planning, strategic thinking, deciding direction and aims, etc. Plan time-slots and personal space for these tasks

When it comes to what the evidence tells us on the issue of prioritisation of time, in my view there is nothing better than the meta-analysis that Viviane Robinson (2011) and her colleagues from the University of Auckland have conducted. The focus of their work was to look at what it is that school leaders do that has the biggest impact on pupil outcomes. The diagram below summarises their findings and identifies the five key activities that leaders undertake that make the biggest difference to pupil outcomes.

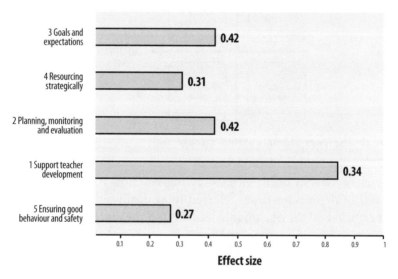

Figure 31: What it is leaders do that has the biggest impact on pupil outcomes
Adapted from Viviane Robinson's *Student-centred leadership*

All of the themes identified in the outcomes above resonate with much we have already covered in this book. But it is striking how the impact of one factor, supporting teacher development, is so much more impactful than its next nearest statistical neighbour. It only goes to show how important it is for leaders at all levels to create the time to focus on helping teachers be better teachers. This most definitely falls into the 'important but not urgent' category in Covey's grid.

Practical ways to use time more effectively

So what can you actually do to manage your time more effectively? To start with, if you can make the time (!) you may want to log how you spend your time over the course of a typical week. This will give you an idea about how much time you spend in each of Covey's quadrants. It can also help you quantify how much of a balance you achieve in each of the three circles in the leadership model below/overleaf. Typically, experience tells me school leaders find their time being sucked into the 'Deliver circle', with insufficient time devoted to the equally important areas of 'Future' and 'Engage'.

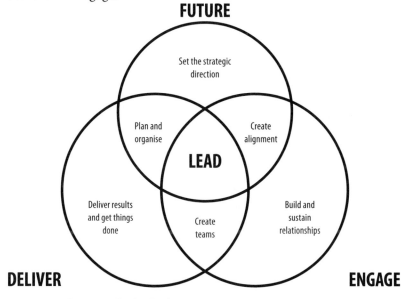

Figure 32: Six key areas for leadership action

Adapted from David Pendleton's Primary Colours model and Steve Radcliffe's Future-Engage-Deliver

Secondly, there are some really simple practical things that can help you and your team. You probably do many of these already. But how ruthless are you in carrying them out? It is precisely when the pressure starts to build that most people tend to throw logic and reason out of the window and just respond to things as they arrive on their desk.

Goal setting

Set yourself goals. These are not the same as to-do lists. They are strategic things you and your team want to achieve in a given time frame. They should drive your overall planning. Break the goals down into small manageable chunks. You need to be realistic when setting your goals. There is nothing more satisfying than meeting a goal and nothing more frustrating than always failing to meet them.

Just say no

If you are one of those people who just can't say 'no', then learn to. You will be surprised how quickly people will find someone else to ask!

Prioritise efficiently

Set up a really efficient system for prioritising your 'live list' of tasks. Given how many tasks can arrive by email, one really easy way to do this is to set up three email folders labelled 'Now, Soon and Later'. You can then use these to place emails into the appropriate box, (not forgetting the option to press delete!) thus keeping your inbox clear. This also allows you to send yourself emails for things that you need to do with the task in the header of the email. The advantage of this system is that all the jobs are in one place. Re-prioritising is easy – you just move emails between the folders. Schedule a short amount of time each day to review your three boxes.

Schedule time for the important but not urgent

It can be really helpful to plan out when you are going to get certain things done. Not only does this help with the temptation to put things off, it also means you can let others know that is what you are doing. This can be important if you find too much of your time is spent dealing with 'incidents' that maybe others can help with on a rota basis. It will also help reduce interruptions, particularly if you combine this with something as simple as saying to your team that if your door is closed you would prefer not to be interrupted.

Avoid procrastination

If you are prone to putting things off, you need to develop ways that help you get down to business. Often, the hardest part is just getting started. There is a school of thought that says you should try and make the very first thing you do each day the thing you are least looking forward to doing. The idea is that you immediately feel pleased once this task is done and are consequently much more efficient and energised than you would be if the job you are dreading were still hanging over you. Try it. It really works! You can also search for 'Eat the Frog' on YouTube to see a short video on this.

Set time limits

If you are prone to just working until the job gets done, you can be sure you will have absolutely no work-life balance. If this is your tendency, set yourself strict time limits and make sure you stick to them. If that means something will have to wait until tomorrow, then so be it.

Delegate more

This is of course, easy to say and hard to do but there are lots of ideas in chapter 10. How often do you ask yourself if someone else could do a particular task? If you do, how often do you decide not to ask someone to do something because you think:

1. Others are just as busy as you are;

2. They aren't paid to do this;

3. They won't do it as well or as quickly as you will;

4. Someone might think you are shirking your responsibilities?

All these reactions are typical and sometimes true. But often people make all kinds of assumptions about what others are thinking or are prepared to do. You will be surprised how carefully chosen tasks, planned in advance, can be seen by others as a great opportunity to develop as well as make an important contribution to the team. The key is not to do this in a way that feels like you are just dumping a problem on someone else at the last minute because you can't be bothered to do it yourself or haven't planned properly.

So effective time management is all about being pro-active in the way you use this precious commodity. Don't allow yourself to be the victim of your circumstances or your own pre-dispositions. Take control and discover how much more is possible when you set yourself some simple but important goals to achieve.

Summary

- Is there a particular change coming up where using the eight-step change model might be helpful for you to use?
- Do you take the time to really think about the different ways individual colleagues respond when a change is happening?
- Do you use data strategically to help you plan?
- Do you take time to properly cost out initiatives?
- Have you taken time to look at what the evidence says about the most effective ways to use the resource available to you?
- Do you know how you actually spend your time?
- What can you do to make more time for those things that are important but not urgent?
- Are there one or two things you can focus on that would enable you to use your time more effectively?

Part 4

Your leadership approach

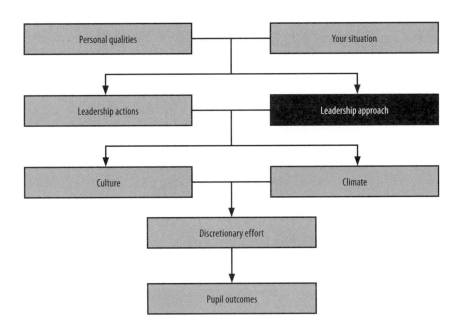

Chapter Thirteen

Your leadership style

It's not what you do (but the way that you do it).
Melvin Oliver and James Young

The previous part of this book focused on the key areas that school leaders need to take action on:

1. Defining the vision and strategic approach

2. Creating alignment

3. Building and sustaining relationships

4. Creating teams

5. Planning and organising

6. Delivering results and getting things done

This part will explore not the *what* but the *how*: your leadership approach. The first chapter will focus on leadership style. The remaining three chapters will look at (i) the importance of transparency, (ii) building trust and (iii) why you should try to develop the habit of *asking first*.

Leadership Style

So what do we mean by leadership style? Why does leadership style matter? Are some leadership styles more effective than others? Daniel Goleman (2000), who is probably best known for his work on emotional intelligence, has also investigated the impact of leadership style on the climate of organisations.

In this work he identified that, as leaders, we tend to use the following six different leadership styles:

Directive (coercive)

Primary objective: compliance. You tend to:

- Give lots of directives, not direction
- Expect immediate staff compliance
- Control tightly
- Rely on negative, corrective feedback
- Motivate by imposing sanctions for non-compliance – with few rewards
- Rarely explains the rationale, only negative consequences

Authoritative (visionary)

Primary objective: providing long-term direction and vision. You tend to:

- Develop and articulate clear vision
- Solicit staff perspective on the vision and see selling the vision as key to success
- Persuade staff by explaining the rationale for the team's best long-term interests
- Set standards and monitor performance in relation to the wider vision
- Motivate with a balance of positive and negative feedback

Affiliative

Primary objective: creating staff harmony. You tend to:

- Be most concerned with promoting friendly interactions
- Place more emphasis on addressing staff needs than on goals and standards

- Pay attention to, and care for, 'the whole person'; stressing things that keep people happy
- Avoid performance-related confrontations
- Reward personal characteristics more than job performance

Democratic
Primary objective: building commitment and generating new ideas. You tend to:

- Trust that staff can develop the appropriate direction for themselves and the school
- Invite all staff to participate in decisions
- Reach decisions by consensus
- Hold many meetings and listen to staff concerns
- Reward adequate performance; rarely give negative feedback

Pace-setting
Primary objective: making rapid progress and achieving tasks to high standards of excellence. You tend to:

- Lead by example and have high standards
- Expect others to know the rationale behind what is being modelled
- Be apprehensive about delegating
- Take responsibility away if high performance is not forthcoming – have little sympathy for poor performance
- Rescue the situation or give detailed task instructions when staff experience difficulties

Coaching
Primary objective: long term professional development of others. You tend to:

- Help staff identify their unique strengths and weaknesses
- Encourage staff to establish long-range development goals
- Reach agreement with staff on the team leader's and individuals' roles in the development process

- Provide on-going advice and feedback
- Trade off immediate standards of performance for long-term development

As you reflect upon the six styles, is there one you tend to use more than the others? Which do you rarely use? Do you make a conscious effort to think about the right approach for any given situation or do you rely on gut instinct?

Leaders at all levels need to be able to use a range of styles to suit their context and any particular situation. The whole of part one of this book stressed the importance of knowing yourself and understanding your situation. Some of your colleagues may require very different handling from others. It's always worth taking time to think about the best way to bring out the best in the individuals in your teams. A competent but unconfident colleague may benefit from a coaching style of leadership. An able but resistant colleague may just need to be told what you expect from them, although in the long run this is probably neither acceptable nor sustainable.

Sometimes a team as a whole can need a very directional approach from a leader, particularly if it isn't functioning particularly well. If you are working with a team of individuals that are not operating as a unit and where performance is very variable, you may just need to say 'we need to do it like this'. Getting basics in place has to be the priority. If the situation you find yourself in is one of disarray, setting clear expectations around behaviour, teaching approaches, marking and homework are all areas where you may just need to be fairly directive to start with.

A high-performing team, however, would find such an approach completely de-motivating. Coming in and telling people what to do would be a disaster. You need to reflect upon the capacity, competence and experience of your team. Knowing which style is best used with the team as a whole, or with different individuals within it, is where your professional judgement and emotional awareness as a leader come in. What is important is that you take the time to consciously think about which approach will build discretionary effort and have the overall impact you are seeking.

In the table below, I have attempted to summarise each of Goleman's six styles and when it might be appropriate to use each.

Style	Description	When useful	Effect size
Visionary	Communicating the goal; expectations on delivery	Pretty much anytime; set pieces and 1:1 dialogue	0.54
Affiliative	Building and sustaining relationships	Again, always useful but especially if morale poor	0.46
Directive	Telling people what to do, often in detail	Low capability or competence; no time	-0.26
Democratic	Sharing decision-making; delegating power	Confidence in the team; more time available	0.43
Pacesetting	Copy me and keep up with me	When need fast change; show what's possible	-0.25
Coaching	Asking questions; focus on developing others	When you have time to build capacity in others	0.42

Figure 33: Summary of different leadership styles and when to use them
Based on Goleman

Daniel Goleman's work also looked at the overall effectiveness of each of the six leadership styles. Whilst there is absolutely a time and a place for each, as the final column of the table above suggests, regardless of the situation, it is true to say that some leadership styles are more effective in their impact on climate than others overall and on average. Goleman identified that the coercive and pacesetting leadership styles had a negative impact on climate in the long term, even though there are times when this is absolutely the right approach to take. This is no surprise in a way. If, as a leader, you find yourself constantly leading by example or telling people what to do because you need to, you are working with people who maybe aren't suited to their roles and need to either improve fast or 'get off the bus'. On the other hand, if you are using these styles but don't actually need to, you will be leading a team who don't feel you trust them and probably feel micro-managed.

As the data above shows, Goleman also identified that the authoritative/ visionary leadership style was, on average, the most effective leadership style overall, closely followed by the democratic, affiliative and coaching styles.

So, taking a moment to think about your leadership approach and, in particular, the right style for your situation, has the potential to make a big difference to the discretionary effort in your team.

Summary

- Have you developed a range of leadership styles that you use flexibly with different colleagues?
- Are there situations or individuals that would benefit from you using a different leadership style?
- Do you tend to just use one or two styles rather than the full range?

Chapter Fourteen

Creating transparency

The truth is like the sun. You can shut it
out for a time but it ain't goin' away.
Elvis Presley

A number of schools I have worked with that have used Jim Collins' work (2001) have been taken by what he would describe as 'confronting the brutal facts whilst never losing faith'. These schools are completely transparent in the way they look at themselves, gather data, share and process that information and then draw conclusions about their next steps. They have completely understood the need to establish the truth of a situation in the school in the strong belief that the right decisions will then become self-evident.

As one school puts it: 'If things are not working, we are encouraged to say so. This is underpinned by openness throughout the system, especially in terms of data and accountability. We work hard to keep things transparent but we try not to use the data or knowledge for blame but as a means to identify and then tackle issues. This has not always been the case, but is something that has evolved as our leadership has become more confident in the reliability of our data.'

Using data and other information to monitor the performance of pupils, individual staff and any team as a whole, is a key part of any leader's role. However such a system is established, it needs to be understood by all staff and not just seen as an accountability tool for the senior team of the school. Of course, accountability is important. There will always remain the need for leaders at all levels to ensure that their staff are performing well and that solid evidence exists to make judgements about colleagues' effectiveness. However, for each team to become truly reflective, there also needs to be a strong professional trust that centres on the information needed to bring about change for the better: better for your pupils, better for your staff and better for your whole school community.

How leaders use data and information

The whole-school systems you put in place need to be evidence-based and evaluative. Schools regularly collect large amounts of data but sometimes fail to use this wealth of information to properly track individual pupil progress, the progress of specific groups or indeed the progress of pupils overall. But the critical condition for success is to create a culture of openness where this information is shared and used not just as a way to judge progress, but also to help the team as a whole, as well as the individuals within it, to develop as professionals.

Thinking about your own team, you need to consider how much of the data that relates to each team member is shared and available to the whole team? Do you create opportunities for your team to use data to help identify individual and team areas to both celebrate and improve on?

Keeping faith

Hopefully your data will tell a story of improvement over time, but this won't always be the case. How you respond to information that paints a less than rosy picture is really important. It can be very tempting for you to bury bad news and carry on in the hope that things will get better. Sometimes they do; but by not really embracing bad news and using it as a way to learn and improve, an opportunity is missed. To paraphrase Jim Collins (2001), the best organisations will always 'confront the brutal facts but keep the faith that something can be done'.

Creating a climate where transparency pervades all of a team's activity is not easy. However, there are a number of practices that you can adopt to support this. Firstly, you can ensure that when you are debating and discussing issues as a team, it is the merit of a particular argument, grounded in data and evidence, that is the basis for decision-making, not the force of personality. This could be a discussion about the best way to teach something or how to set up a whole-school initiative on literacy. Using data and other evidence to support the decision-making process depersonalises the arguments and usually leads to better decision-making.

Secondly, when things go wrong, examination of the reasons why this happened needs to be conducted in a 'no-blame' way. This is about you creating a climate where experimentation and learning from mistakes is encouraged. For example, if an idea to introduce lunchtime catch-up classes doesn't seem to be having the impact you had hoped for, or if the change of syllabus you have introduced in your own department or one you line manage hasn't led to the increase in results you had anticipated, what is needed is a 'what went wrong and how can we work together to improve the situation' approach, rather than 'who's bad idea was it to do that?' Once again, the focus is not on who is responsible for a particular situation having arisen, but what the facts of the matter are that the team can learn from.

Thirdly, you need to make sure that there is an openness in the way decisions are made and communicated. When you are allocating resources, deciding who works with which groups of pupils or how work is allocated amongst the team, try to work to an agreed set of principles that everyone can see are being fairly applied. Nothing is more divisive than colleagues thinking that a leader, at any level, has favourites or hidden agendas when it comes to making appointments or writing the timetable, for example.

Responding to unwelcome news

Paradoxically, a charismatic leader can sometimes work against creating a culture of transparency. A strong leader, who everyone wants to please, may be exactly the kind of person to whom it is very difficult to bring bad news. Hearing that behaviour is becoming a bit of a concern, for example, can sometimes be the last thing a leader wants someone to tell them, even though they know it is important. Of course, how you as a leader respond to challenging information brought to you by an individual is important. If you give a defensive or irritated response, this will obviously tend to deter someone from raising issues again. But equally unhelpful is for your response to be to ignore the feedback and take no action. In either case, it is unlikely that person will bring up difficult issues again.

To sum up, highly successful teams operate in a climate and culture where information, data and decision-making are shared openly and used supportively. These teams have 100% confidence in their own ability to bring about the changes needed. In other words, they keep faith in their own capacity to overcome difficulties even in challenging circumstances. This resilience and inner strength comes from a sense of common purpose and collaborative endeavour supported by strong and highly effective leadership that inspires the necessary confidence and self-belief.

Summary

- How open are you with data and other information?
- How good are you at doing the right thing, based on evidence and data?
- How good are you at confronting the brutal facts but keeping faith in your ability to overcome them?

Chapter Fifteen

Building trust

The first thing we build is trust.
Bouygues: French construction company

Collaboration and partnership are both phrases commonly heard in schools. Whilst these are crucial elements of any school's success, it is probably true to say that many educationalists talk about partnership working and co-operation without really taking time to consider the conditions that allow for such effective practice to take place or what it actually looks like in reality.

It is really important not to overlook the importance of creating a climate of trust where you are able to concentrate your energies and talents reaching your goals, rather than spending time engaged in unproductive and misdirected activity associated with concerns about others' motives and unnecessary bureaucracy.

In his book *Speed of Trust*, Stephen Covey (2008) sets out why building trust is so important for the success of any organisation. In his view, where levels of trust are low, staff will be working in an unproductive environment, often associated with unrest and where they are often divided into political camps. It's an environment where bureaucracy slows down productivity and creates low levels of innovation and development. Inevitably, discretionary effort is low.

In teams with a high level of trust, systems and procedures are helpfully aligned and bureaucracy is kept to a minimum. Individuals are trusted and supported to carry out their work. There are positive and transparent relationships amongst staff, leading to innovation, confidence and loyalty. Discretionary effort is high.

How do you build trust as a leader?

Stephen Covey argues, and I agree, that there are three key elements to people trusting you.

Firstly, people need to know you have faith in them and care about their success as individuals. Finding ways, through the use of praise and feedback, to let people know when you think they are doing a great job is the easiest way to do this.

Secondly, people need to know they can trust your integrity. Do you respect their confidence when they share personal or sensitive information? Do you avoid over-promising so you can always do what you say you are going to do, even when this is difficult? Do you treat everyone fairly?

Thirdly, and often overlooked, do people need to have trust in your competence and judgement? Your staff need to be confident that you know what you are doing, even if inside you don't feel like you do! One easy step, however, is to lead by example on things you are asking others to do. Not only is this an excellent way to influence others, it helps create the culture of 'how we do things around here' as well as building confidence in your ability to deliver. I am not advocating you do this all the time, but it is a powerful way of building trust. It is also really important to make sure you regularly reflect on your strengths and weaknesses as a leader and work systematically and consistently on building on those areas of strength as well as addressing those areas you need to improve.

Exemplifying trust is an important symbol

Some of the examples that follow may appear to be somewhat simplistic, but they do demonstrate – in a very straightforward way – where institutions have high levels of trust.

Teams with a high level of trust will not have systems and procedures that are about always checking up on people. For example, if the head of a curriculum area requires their team to submit their lesson plans to them on a daily basis, their team is likely to feel that the quality of their work and the level of their professionalism is in question. This is in no way to undermine the importance of the support that new entrants into the profession will need with lesson planning. Nor is it suggesting that peer-to-peer sharing of ideas is unhelpful. Where a trust is undermined is where there is an implicit suggestion that someone cannot be trusted to complete work to an appropriate standard unless it is going to be checked.

Schools where the locking of doors is deemed unnecessary by staff shows a high level of basic trust between all staff and pupils. Of course, there will be times when this trust is undermined by a particular individual, but a school that has the confidence in itself and all the people who work there to leave doors unlocked sends a clear message to everyone. Not only that, the time wasted when someone needs to enter a space that is locked and they don't have the key is a classic example of where a lack of trust can slow up proceedings and reduce productivity, motivation and effectiveness.

Another key indicator of a high-trust school relates to processes for delegation, which were examined in more detail in chapter 10. Clearly, good leaders will often delegate tasks. However, to maintain high levels of trust, it is essential that once something has been delegated, the person concerned is left to carry out the task they have been given. It can be very tempting to ask or advise a colleague about what is being done throughout the process. This can actually create more work overall, make the person feel undervalued or not trusted, and is generally unproductive.

In low-risk situations, it is sometimes better to allow a colleague to fail to complete a given task satisfactorily and then go back through it afterwards. The learning that can emerge is often far more powerful than if there had been an earlier intervention. Of course, if the person doesn't have the necessary skills or experience to cope with the task they have been delegated then they are unfortunately being set up to fail. Part of the skill of a good school leader is knowing when is the right time to delegate, making sure that colleagues know they can ask for advice if they need to without any negative value judgement being made about their abilities.

Trusting pupils

Although the principle applies in all contexts, for leaders in a pastoral role, showing your pupils you trust them is very powerful, although the principle applies in all contexts. For example, giving your pupil or student council a proper remit to consider issues that go beyond school dinners or the toilets is important. Do they have the chance to help you appoint staff? Are they trusted to input on financial decisions? Some schools give councils a small budget with which they can prioritise areas for spending. What other leadership roles do you create for pupils? If you have a curriculum responsibility, how much do you seek and trust the views of pupils about the quality of provision? In both primary and secondary phases, pupils can be surprisingly astute when it comes to making judgements about the quality of the deal they getting.

The speed of trust

Finally, it is just worth considering how quickly trust can be built and how quickly it can be destroyed. Interestingly, Stephen Covey suggests this isn't the same for each of the elements.

When it comes to people trusting competence, this can be established pretty quickly. In a modest way, you can discreetly make others aware of your track record. If you have been promoted internally this may not even be necessary. You can also ensure some quick wins that make everyone feel confident that you know what you are doing. This element of trust is also usually slow to decline. People tend to cut you a bit of slack in the short term if something goes wrong, although you clearly need to make sure this doesn't become too regular an event!

When it comes to your personal integrity, however, precisely the opposite is true. It can take a while for people to know they can trust you to keep confidences, for examples. This aspect usually needs 'testing' before your colleagues will trust you. They need to know from experience. Conversely, your integrity can be destroyed in an instant if you are found to have been dishonest about something or gossiped about something private. Keeping this in mind is critical, as for some people if this happens it can mean they will never trust you again.

So, to summarise, building trust has a significant impact on the culture and climate of any team. There are three key elements for you to keep in mind: showing faith and care for the success of others; your own personal integrity; and your perceived competence and track record.

Summary

How could you find out about perceived levels of trust from your teams?

If you identify there is a need to build trust, what are the actions you might undertake as a priority?

Chapter Sixteen

Asking First

Listening is a positive act. You have
to put yourself out to do it.
David Hockney

In the end, leadership is about developing the right habits. As a school leader, I suspect you will be achieving your successes through a whole range of habits you don't even know you have. This final chapter looks at one leadership habit that I think underpins pretty much everything this book has been about: 'asking first'. If you want to understand yourself and your context better, you need to ask questions of yourself, others and your context. You need to interrogate or ask questions of the data you have at your disposal. Only by doing this are you in a position to identify *what* you need to make your priorities for actions. And only then can you decide on *how* you will implement these priorities: your leadership approach.

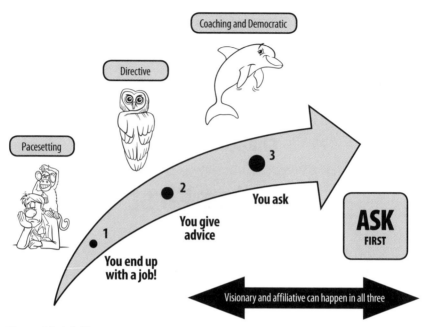

Figure 34: Ask First

Based on over 20 years in a whole range of senior leadership roles, I think school leaders at all levels only have three types of conversation!

'Monkey on the shoulder' conversations

In the first type, someone comes to talk to you about an issue and concern. Before you know it, you've ended up with a job! I call these your 'monkey on the shoulder' conversations where the monkey has quickly jumped from them onto you. Of course, there is a time and place where this is appropriate. If something is high-risk and looking like it is about to go wrong, you may well need to step in. If a colleague is really stressed out for some reason and just can't cope, you need to help. But if your habit is to take on jobs from others without thinking, you aren't really leading, you are just doing.

I can remember as a young head of year, letting a huge number of monkeys jump on my back. Looking back there were a number of reasons why this tended to happen: firstly because I genuinely wanted to help out someone who I thought was very busy; secondly, because

I wanted the other person to think I was capable and good at my job; thirdly, because it just felt quicker and easier to do something myself; and finally, because the reality of the culture in my school at that time was that heads of year were seen as firefighters, not team leaders. But as the thickness of the arrow on the model implies, whilst there is a place for type one conversations, you shouldn't have too many.

'Wise owl' conversations

The second type of conversation also has its place. These are dialogues in which you end up giving advice, making suggestions or even just telling someone what to do. At least with these, you don't end up with the job! Hopefully, the other person will be able to apply what they have learnt in the conversation in the future. But if they keep coming back to you with similar questions, and if you continue to just answer them, they can become over-dependent upon you when it comes to making decisions or deciding what to do. These conversations don't build capacity or competence in your colleagues. In fact, they do the reverse.

'Dolphin' conversations

The third type of conversation, and the important habit I am suggesting all leaders need to keep developing, is that of 'asking first'. In type three conversations, leaders just ask brilliant questions. Initially, these help you understand the situation; both the context and an individual's capacity to manage it. Only then can you decide the best way to proceed. If at this point you identify that you need to intervene and take the job off them or give them advice, then that's fine. You have made a conscious decision to do that. Not because it's what you are predisposed to do, but because it's what the situation needs.

Of course, if you both have time, spending a tiny bit longer on the conversation and staying in questioning mode can very often help people work out for themselves what they need to do. These mini-coaching conversations don't have to take long. It is more about you using a coaching leadership style than it is actually formally coaching. In a nutshell what you should aim to do is ask questions that help the other person to:

1. Clarify what they want to achieve (the **g**oal)

2. Understand all the factors that are relevant to the context (the **r**eality);

3. Consider the various options available to them (the **o**ptions);

4. Decide what to do (what they **w**ill do).

As the letters in bold above highlight, this simple approach to structuring these conversations uses one of the most well know coaching acronyms, GROW, which was created by John Whitmore (2009).

You will be surprised, even in a one-minute conversation, how much of this ground can be covered. You leave the conversation with no task to undertake. Your colleague leaves feeling they have been properly listened to and having had the opportunity to think through the situation. They are also less likely to ask you the same question again next time.

The link with Goleman's research
Daniel Goleman's (2001) work on leadership styles that we examined in chapter 13 is directly relevant here and lends some evidence in support of my "Ask First" model. If you think about it, in type one conversations you are pretty much adopting a pace-setting leadership style. Type two broadly relates to you being coercive or directive. Both of these, on average and over time, were shown to have a negative effect on organisational performance where leaders overly relied upon them. However, type three conversations are much more akin to the democratic and coaching leadership styles, both of which, the evidence suggests, have a positive effect over time.

Of course there are times when coercive or pacesetting leadership is required, often in times of crisis when colleagues will look to you as leader for guidance and direction. However, over time, the most effective leaders shift from leading in front of the team to leading the team from within.

The importance of listening
As David Hockney reminds us in his quote from the beginning of this chapter, 'Listening is a positive act. You have to put yourself out to do it'. Even if you have developed the habit of asking great questions, if you don't listen actively, you will be missing the opportunity to be even more effective. It is not about being soft. Listening to colleagues can tell you important information about what is really happening on the ground, it

provides room for your team to grow and develop their thinking and it is more likely to lead to distributed and sustainable leadership.

The first thing about listening is that it is active not passive. When done well, listening gives you more information about a situation or individual, and leads you towards greater insight, awareness or learning. You might see a different perspective or clarify your thinking. Active listening relies on good questioning. By structuring your questions, you can lead someone through a thinking process or suggest new ways of approaching a problem. How well do you tend to structure your questions at the moment? Are they leading or open? Do they provide enough space for the other person to reflect? Do your questions build on one another to lead to deeper learning?

You can also listen and pick up information that goes beyond the words the other person is using. You can listen for emotion, body language, tone of voice, speed of talking and clarity of thinking. Listening actively, these will tell you a great deal about the other person's frame of mind, emotional state and the purpose of the conversation. Often the words someone is using do not reflect what they really mean or want to say. How far do you listen beyond the words for what is really behind a conversation, what isn't being said?

How to show you are listening
Others are more likely to share if they feel that you are listening to them or that listening is resulting in some action or change. To a certain extent the relevance of your questions will demonstrate that you are listening. Techniques you can use to show listening are reflecting back the words someone has used or making statements showing you understand their emotions. Your body language and tone of voice can also mirror the non-verbal signals that they are giving. If they are angry you might choose to change your body language or tone of voice so it is non-confrontational; if they are upset, you might again change it to elicit a different response.

Four levels of listening
The importance of actively listening is summarised well in Julie Starr's (2002) four levels of listening model below. The further down the model you go the better your listening and the more productive the outcomes.

Level	Activity of listener	What other person thinks
1. Attending	Eye contact and body language show interest	This person wants to listen to me
2. Accurate listening	Above – plus accurate paraphrasing of what other says	This person hears and understands what I am talking about
3. Empathetic listening	All of above – plus matching non-verbal cues with metaphor use & own feelings	This person knows what it feels like to be in my situation
4. Generative empathetic listening	All of above – plus the ability to use intuition & feelings to connect more fully & deeply with other person's situation	This person helps me to hear myself more fully than I can by myself – without telling me what to do, is helping me to find my own way.

Figure 35: Levels of Listening
Adapted from *The coaching manual*, Julie Starr

So this final chapter has focused on two key, inter-related leadership habits: asking first and listening well. If the success of great school leadership depends on understanding context and situation and using this knowledge to determine what you need to do and how you need to do it, I hope you can see why I have chosen to end with these key skills. I know from my own experience as a school leader and from the hundreds of leaders I have worked with, that spending time on consciously improving your proficiency in these areas will pay dividends.

To conclude, I do hope this book has provided you with a comprehensive set of practical tools you can use in school, underpinned by a useful theoretical framework. May I wish you all success in your leadership roles, both now and in the future!

Summary

1. Are you aware the balance of type 1, 2 and 3 conversations you have?

2. Do you already have the habit of *asking first* or is this something you want to focus on?

3. Do you actively listen in conversations?

4. Do you show others that you are listening?

Key references

Ancona, D et al (2007) *The incomplete leader.* Harvard Business Review: hbr.org.

Black, P and William, D (1998) *Inside the black box* NFER – Nelson.

Bambrick-Santoyo, P (2012) *Leverage Leadership: a practical guide to building exceptional schools.* San Francisco: Jossey-Bass.

Brighouse, T (2007). *How successful head teachers survive and thrive.* [Online] RM, Available at: www.rm.com.

Brighouse, T and Woods, D (2008). *What makes a good school now?* Network Continuum.

Campbell, A (2015) *Winners: And how they succeed.* London: Hutchinson.

Clough, P and Strycharczyk, D (2012). *Developing Mental Toughness: Improving Performance, Wellbeing and Positive Behaviour in Others.* London: Kogan Page.

Coffield, F., Moseley, D., Hall, E., Ecclestone, K. (2004). *Learning styles and pedagogy in post-16 learning. A systematic and critical review.* London: Learning and Skills Research Centre.

Collins, J (2001). *Good to great.* U.S.A: Collins Business.

Covey, S (2008) *The speed of trust. One thing that changes everything.* London: Simon and Schuster.

Covey, S (2004) *7 habits of highly effective people.* London: Simon and Schuster.

Drucker, P (2007) *Essential Drucker: management, the individual and society* Routledge.

Dudley, P (2014) *Lesson study: professional learning for our time.* New York: Routledge.

Dweck, C (2012) *Mindset: How You Can Fulfil Your Potential.* U.S.A: Ballantine Books.

Education Endowment Foundation (EEF) (2015) *Making the best use of teaching assistants* Available from: educationedowmentfoundation.org.uk.

Education Endowment Foundation (2014) *Teaching and Learning Toolkit.* Available from: educationendowmentfoundation.org.uk/toolkit/toolkit-a-z/

Fullan, M (2001) *Leading the culture of change*. Jossey-Bass.

Fullan, M (2008a) *The six secrets of change*. Jossey-Bass.

Goleman, D (2002) *The new leaders*. Little, Brown.

Goleman, D (2000). *Leadership that gets results*. Harvard Business Review March-April 2000.

Goleman, D (1995) *Emotional Intelligence: Why it Can Matter More Than IQ*. London: Bloomsbury.

Heifetz, R and Linsky, M (2002) *Leadership on the Line: Staying Alive through the Dangers of Leading*. U.S.A: Harvard Business School Press.

Handy, C (1997) *The hungry spirit*. Hutchinson.

Hattie, J (2009) *Visible Learning: A Synthesis of Over 800 Meta-Analyses Relating to Achievement*. New York: Routledge.

Hargreaves, D (2011) *Leading a self-improving school system: towards maturity*. [online] NCSL. Available from: dera.ioe.ac.uk/15804/1/a-self-improving-school-system-towards-maturity.pdf

Hay Group (2007) *Rush to the top: Accelerating the development of leaders in schools* [online]. Available from: www.haygroup.com/downloads/uk/Rush_to_the_Top_low_res.pdf

Kilmann, R et al (1994) *Producing useful knowledge for organisations*. San Francisco: Jossey-Bass.

Kotter, J P (1996) *Leading change*. USA: Harvard Business Review Press.

Kübler-Ross, E (1969) *On death and dying*. New York: Scribner.

Leithwood, K et al (2007) *Seven strong claims about successful school leadership*. National College of School Leadership.

Lencioni, P M (2002) *The five dysfunctions of a team; a leadership fable*. San Francisco: Jossey-Bass.

Lencioni, P M (2012) *The advantage*. San Francisco: Jossey-Bass.

Luft, J Ingham, H (1955) *The Johari window, a graphic model of interpersonal awareness*. Los Angeles: University of California.

Matthews, P (2009) *Twelve outstanding secondary schools*. Ofsted.

Mehrabian, A (1972) *Nonverbal Communication*. New Brunswick: Aldine Transaction

National Governors' Association (NGA) (2015) *A Framework for Governance* Available at: http://www.nga.org.uk/Services/ConsultancyandTraining/Being-strategic/A-Framework-for-Governance.aspx

NCSL (2003) *Heart of the matter: a practical guide to what middle leaders can do to improve learning in secondary schools* [online]. Available from: webarchive.nationalarchives.gov.uk/tna/20140701125459/http:/nationalcollege.org.uk/docinfo?id=17209&filename=heart-of-the-matter.pdf

NCSL (2004) *A model of school leadership in challenging urban environments*. NCSL.

Pendleton, D and Furnham, A (2012) *Leadership: all you need to know.* Great Britain: Palgrave Macmillan.

Radcliffe, S (2012) (2nd ed). *Leadership: plain and simple.* Edinburgh: Pearson.

Reynolds, D (2004) *Within-school variation: its extent and causes.* DfES.

Robinson, V (2011) *Student centred leadership.* Jossey-Bass.

Scott, S (2003) *Fierce conversations.* U.S.A: Piatkus books Ltd.

Starr, J (2002) *The coaching manual.* London: Pearson.

Strong, M et al (2011) *Experiments in the identification of successful teachers.* USA: Journal of Teacher education.

Tuckman, Bruce (1965) *Developmental sequence in small groups.* Psychological Bulletin 63 (6): 384–99. doi:10.1037/h0022100.

Ward, S. (2009) *Time management types* [online]. Available from: sbinfocanada.about. com/cs/timemanagement/a/timetypes.htm

Watkins, M (2003) *The first 90 days.* Harvard Business Review publications: HBR.org

Whitmore, J (2009) *Coaching for performance GROWing Human Potential and Purpose – the Principles and Practice of Coaching and Leadership* (4th Ed). London: Nicholas Brealy Publishing.

Dylan, Wiliam, *Times Educational Supplement article* 10th April 2015.

Acknowledgment

Sincere thanks to James Toop and Oli Tomlinson for their great contributions to particular chapters and to Rachel Macfarlane and Barbara Taylor for their painstaking proof-reading of the book. It has become apparent that my use of commas leaves a lot to be desired.

Also by the same author

The Art of Standing Out

Transforming Your School to Outstanding ... and Beyond

By Andrew Morrish

The Art of Standing Out is a powerful, must-read blueprint for Heads, leadership teams and governors at schools with world-class ambitions.

It is the culmination of 18 years' experience as a headteacher for Andrew Morrish, who has led two schools from 'special measures' to 'outstanding'.

As a founder CEO of a successful MAT, National Leader of Education, speaker and blogger, Andrew shows readers clearly and simply how it is possible to create a stand-out school.

Drawing on Andrew's time as Head, The Art of Standing Out is a unique blend of personal insights and tried-and-tested strategies to help school leaders create schools that are celebrated far beyond simple Ofsted categorisation.

High Challenge, Low Threat

Finding the balance

By Mary Myatt

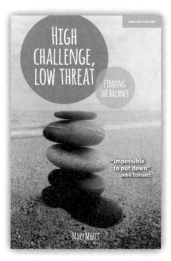

High Challenge, Low Threat is Mary Myatt's smart and thoughtful exploration of all the things that wise leaders do.

Informed through thousands of conversations over a 20-year career in education, Mary shows the lessons that school management teams can learn from leaders in a wide range of other sectors and points to the conditions which these leaders create to allow colleagues to engage with difficult issues enthusiastically and wholeheartedly.

This compassionate book makes the case that any leadership role is concerned primarily with the relationships between individuals. It is the quality of these, whatever the size of the organisation, which make the difference between organisations which thrive, and those which stagnate.

This is not to argue for soft, easy and comfortable options. Instead it considers how top leaders manage to walk the line between the impossible and the possible, between the undoable and the doable, and to create conditions for productive work which transcend the difficulties which come towards us every day. Instead of dodging them, they embrace them.

And by navigating high challenge, low threat, they show how others how to do the same.